Change and Continuity

Change and Continuity

Tennessee Politics
since the Civil War

William R. Majors

MERCER

ISBN 0-86554-209-0

Change and Continuity
Copyright © 1986
Mercer University Press, Macon, Georgia 31207
All rights reserved
Printed in the United States of America

The paper used in this publication meets the minimum requirements
of American National Standard for Information Sciences—
Permanence of Paper for Printed Library Materials, ANSI Z39.48-1984.

Library of Congress Cataloging-in-Publication Data
Majors, William R., 1929–1986.
Change and continuity.
Bibliography: p. 121.
Includes index.
1. Tennessee—Politics and government—1865–1950.
2. Tennessee—Politics and government—1951–   .
I. Title.
F436.M24   1986   976.8'05   86-12523
ISBN 0-86554-209-0 (alk. paper)

Contents

To Marcia

Preface

The American South, from the early days of the republic, has been regarded as a separate cultural region. Almost from the beginning, fascinated social observers have sought to determine the region's distinctive features. Thus scholars have identified the "mind of the South," the "idea of the South," and the historic "central theme," and so on. All attempts to interpret Southern distinctiveness ultimately run against one fundamental fact: the South is not a huge cultural monolith. There are many Souths. Indeed, geographical variations alone have produced richly diverse cultural patterns. Not only are there regional variations, the South is also divided politically into many parts. There are similarities among the parts but each is uniquely different in many respects from the others. The real South is therefore elusive of precise interpretation.

The South has also been an ever-changing land. In fact, every generation has experienced such profound change that contemporary observers believed that the region was losing its distinctiveness and was about to enter the cultural mainstream of the nation. These epithets for Dixie were, however, invariably more hopeful than accurate. To be sure, certain dramatic events and movements did indeed alter Southern cultural patterns to some degree. Scholars, preoccupied with trying to determine the extent to which the patterns were reshaped, have all too often overreached and exaggerated the change. To paraphrase an astute observation once made by Barbara Tuchman on an entirely different subject, the scholars found what they expected to find even if it was not always there. Eventually, after closer examination and reflection, interpreters

were forced to admit that the alleged alterations in cultural patterns produced by great events and trends were, more often than
not, more apparent than real. On the contrary, they discovered that
underlying Southern social norms, values, and beliefs defied change
or threats of change and confirmed the "everlasting South" thesis
of Francis Butler Simpkins. In sum, then, there is a real South but
there are also many Souths and it is a region of change and continuity.

It is no great exaggeration to suggest that each Southern state
is the South in miniature. Within each state, to a greater or lesser
degree, there are physical and cultural variations similar to the
Southern region as a whole. There is no better example of this internal diversity than the state of Tennessee. Not over one hundred
twelve miles at its widest point from north to south, the state is a
narrow ribbon stretching more than four hundred miles from a
high in the Appalachian Mountains in the east to the banks of the
Mississippi River in the west. The geographical differences within
the Volunteer State are so great that the state's fundamental law and
statutes recognize three Grand Divisions: East, Middle, and West
Tennessee. East Tennessee is an area of high mountains and long
valleys and is separated from the middle section by the Cumberland Plateau. Middle Tennessee consists of the Central Basin, an
area of plains, rolling hills, and river bottom lands, surrounded by
the Highland Rim. The dividing line between the middle section
and West Tennessee is the Tennessee River in the west. The western region is almost equally divided between rolling hill country
bordering the Tennessee River and plains bordering the Mississippi River.

Historically, Tennessee's problems have been similar to those
of the other Southern states. But the cultural patterns also differed. The Volunteer State has been classified as an "upper South"
or "border" state. This suggests that the social institutions of Tennessee, along with Kentucky, North Carolina, and Virginia differed from those in the "lower" or "deep" South. The classification
has some merit. Generally, race was never as pervasive an issue in
the upper South as in the deep South and the Republican party,
although a minority, was stronger in the border South. But Tennessee's experiences also differed from sister upper South states.

The state is a mixture or cross-section of the entire South. Because both soil and terrain were not suited for large-scale agriculture, East Tennessee was populated by small farmers. Cultural development was almost identical to the mountainous regions of adjacent states. In contrast, plantation agriculture took hold on the plains of the western part of the state in the antebellum era. Consequently, West Tennessee had more slaves and that region's cultural patterns were like those in the lower South. The political, economic, and social evolution in Middle Tennessee was more like that of the western than the eastern section.

The variations in geography and patterns of settlement in Tennessee resulted in a diverse economy and social-class structure in the state. Although originally agricultural, the state's economy, especially after the Civil War, began a gradual transformation from agrarian to industrial and from rural to urban. Social classes included small farmers and planters, small town and urban merchants and professionals, and industrial managers and workers. Tennessee's cultural multiplicity may well be the reason why the Volunteer State's responses to events, issues, trends, and reform movements were normally moderate. The agrarian revolt of the 1890s, for example, did not spawn a radical leader and race-baiting politicians were never successful statewide. Tennessee's experiences have thus been both like and unlike the rest of the South.

This volume traces briefly Tennessee politics from the Civil War to the present, identifying changes resulting from trends, movements, and important events as well as continuity. The basic assumption here is that in the century and a quarter from the onset of the Civil War, the state's political institution has been confronted almost continuously with change or threats of change from both national and state issues. Indeed change has occurred; both the physical and cultural environments have been altered appreciably. The hypothesis of this volume posits that despite the enormous changes in both the physical and cultural landscape in Tennessee since the Civil War, a basic cultural pattern, a set of norms, values, and beliefs, or more specifically a Bourbon conservatism has persisted relatively unaltered; that a community of interests, when faced with change or threats of change, adjusted or accommodated to change, reconciling progress with tradition. Tennessee's experience in change has been both like and unlike the rest of the South. Its experience in continuity, however, may be an important clue to a better understanding of the American South as a distinct cultural region.

In writing this study, I have been influenced by my own research in the primary materials, the manuscripts and papers relative to the state. I have also relied heavily on secondary sources and on the work of eminent scholars in the field of Southern history and especially from in-depth studies on Tennessee. It is therefore not entirely original in interpretation. Some interpretations may have been carried to a greater extreme than was intended by those from whom they were borrowed. For this, I apologize. I hope, however, that this volume will prove to be useful to those seeking a better understanding of the state's historical evolution as well as the present cultural environment. I welcome challenges to my thesis and I will be pleased if my efforts stimulate more in-depth probing of the cultural milieu in the Volunteer State. Tennessee, especially in the twentieth century, is almost virgin soil for scholarly exploration.

I am once again deeply indebted to my wife, Lynelle Vickers Majors for enduring with patience the long periods of neglect that so often occurs in the preparation of a manuscript. I, of course, assume full responsibility for all errors of fact and interpretation, real or imagined.

Chapter 1

Civil War, Reconstruction, and Redemption

It was long assumed that the Civil War, as the watershed event delineating the "Old South" from the "New South," radically reshaped Southern society. Thus in the case of Tennessee, V. O. Key, Jr., in his monumental study, *Southern Politics in State and Nation*, argued that politics in the Volunteer State in the twentieth century were the result of geographical diversity and "patterns of political behavior deposited by the Civil War." Very simply, because Middle and West Tennessee had more slaves and favored secession in 1861, those sections became Democratic in the postwar years, and because the eastern section had few slaves and preferred to remain in the Union, that region became predominantly Republican. From a superficial view, the Civil War seemed indeed to have been responsible for Tennessee's latter-day party makeup, but historical developments are seldom so simple and linear. Historians in recent years have demonstrated conclusively that alterations wrought by the upheaval of the war were at best, minimal. Changes in Tennessee's political structure were not monumental by any means.

In the generation before the Civil War, a viable two-party system developed in the Volunteer State as the Jacksonian Democracy and the Whig party contested for political domination. According to the conventional view, Democrats were agrarian, advocates of states' rights and opposed to tariff protection, a national bank, and internal improvements financed by the federal government. In contrast, Whigs were business minded and favored a protective tariff, a national bank, and were willing to accept federal subsidies for commerce and industry. Although there may have been tendencies within both parties to adhere to these principles, Tennessee's Democrats and Whigs did not fit the stereotypes. The Whig party, for example, did not originate in differences over economic or philosophical issues. Rather, Whiggery rose as the result of personal rivalries and contests over power and spoils during Andrew Jackson's ascendancy. Both parties were essentially conservative and both claimed to be the true advocate of Jeffersonian democracy. Nevertheless, the parties were so evenly matched that they exchanged control of the governorship seven times between 1835 and 1853. Although Whigs seemed to be a bit stronger in East Tennessee and the Democratic party in a slight majority in the middle and western sections, each had significant pockets of strength in every section and many counties in each region were evenly balanced. There is no satisfactory explanation for the inconsistent party makeup in pre-Civil War Tennessee. Thomas B. Alexander noted that neither geography nor economic factors such as slaveholding, business enterprise, and urbanization explained party domination of any county or section. Comparisons of party-controlled areas "reveal only tendencies—with important exceptions." Many factors, "including personalities, went into the making" of Tennessee's complicated party system. Although the Whig party as a national organization died in the 1850s, Whiggery was still strong in Tennessee on the eve of the Civil War.

As the crisis over slavery deepened, it became clear that the presidential election in 1860 would be crucial. The four-way race was a contest of extremes. On the one hand, the Republican candidate, Abraham Lincoln, constituted a threat to the very existence of slavery. At the other extreme, a Southern Democrat, John Cabell Breckinridge, was supported by the "fire-eaters," open advocates of secession. A Northern Democrat, Stephen Arnold Douglas, a moderate, stood for preserving the Union through popular sovereignty. The recently organized Constitutional Union party, made up largely of former Whigs and Know Nothings, nominated Tennessee native and ex-Whig John Bell. Although conservative, the new party took a more moderate stance between the extremes, damned both "fire-eaters" and antislavery agitators, and advocated preserving the Union through compromise and reconciliation. The outcome of the presidential election revealed that the sentiment in Tennessee ranged from moderate conservatism to reaction. Bell, with traditional Whig votes, carried the state narrowly. He won East Tennessee by a majority and West Tennessee by a plurality. Breckinridge took the middle section by a small margin. Douglas was a poor third in all sections and Lincoln had no recorded vote. The deep Southern states, however, would not accept the winner in the presidential contest, Lincoln, and, led by South Carolina, began the process of secession. By February 1861, the Confederacy had been established. Tennessee was therefore faced with the agonizing decision of remaining in the Union or joining the Southern cause.

In the weeks following South Carolina's withdrawal from the Union, Tennesseans became involved in an intense, often bitter debate over secession. Although there were important exceptions, Whigs tended to be loyalists. Many, both Whig and Democrat, urged the state to take a "wait and see" position. Advocates of secession were led by "fire-eating" Democratic governor, Isham Green Harris. The governor proposed that the General Assembly determine the popular will through a plebiscite. The legislature responded and set a referendum for early February 1861. The state rejected secession by some nine thousand votes out of approximately 127,000 cast. East Tennessee voted to remain in the Union, West Tennessee favored secession, and the middle section was evenly divided.

Although secession was voted down, the result was not a mandate for unionism. Agitation for separation continued and when President Lincoln, after the firing on Fort Sumter in April, issued a call for 75,000 volunteers to put down the rebellion, sentiment in Tennessee shifted dramatically. The use of force to prevent secession was repugnant to many loyalists. Governor Harris began preparations for joining the Confederacy and the General Assembly called another referendum to be held 8 June 1861. For the second time East Tennessee rejected secession by a two to one margin but the middle and western sections voted overwhelmingly for withdrawal from the Union. Thus Tennessee was committed to the Confederacy and preparations were made to fight in defense of the South. Many Unionist Whigs in the middle and western regions reluctantly acquiesced in the decision and indeed some served in the Confederate Army or took positions in the Confederate government. East Tennessee was bitter over the commitment to the Confederacy. Whigs, allied with Union Democrats in that section petitioned for permission to form a separate state, a request that was denied by the General Assembly. Tennessee thus joined the Southern cause and participated in the Civil War against the passionate opposition from the eastern region.

The Civil War left a legacy of bitterness that lasted for more than a generation after the conflict was over. The issues of secession and war divided families, friends, neighbors, and entire communities all across the state. Anger at Tennessee's separation was especially acute in East Tennessee and was no doubt a factor in individual feuding and conflict that sometimes resulted in bloodshed. The state also suffered from the horrors of war for it became a major battleground; only in Virginia were more battles fought. Ironically, the sections favoring secession were overrun by Union forces early while East Tennessee remained in the hands of the Confederacy for two years.

Because of its geographic location Tennessee was a major target for the Union offensive in the west. In addition, three rivers, one on the western boundary and two flowing across the state, were convenient highways for attack. The first Confederate line of defense ran across Kentucky from west to east just north of Tennessee. Two important posts guarding rivers were just inside the state's line, Fort Henry on the Tennessee River and Fort Donelson on the Cumberland River. These forts were the initial objectives in the first Union attack in the west which began in February 1862 and both fell quickly. The defense line had thus been penetrated and the remainder of the line began to collapse. Fearing that Nashville could not be defended, the commanding Confederate general abandoned the city and retired across Tennessee to northern Alabama. Governor Harris and members of the state government fled Nashville, first to Memphis and then to Mississippi where they remained in exile. As units of the Union army occupied Tennessee's capital city, General Ulysses Simpson Grant moved a large force up the Tennessee River to Hardin County on the Mississippi line. In April, at Shiloh, in one of the bloodiest battles in the war, the Confederates attacked Grant in an effort to turn back the Union advance. The attempt failed and Southern forces were compelled to retreat into Mississippi. Meanwhile, another Union army was advancing down the Mississippi River, and in June took Memphis. By the end of 1862, despite Confederate attacks in Middle Tennessee, all of West Tennessee and a large portion of the middle section, including Nashville, were in federal hands. In 1863, the Union began an advance to the southeast of Nashville that culminated in the taking of Chattanooga and the conquest of East Tennessee. The Volunteer State was, by the end of 1863, conquered territory. The Union's military successes necessitated the early establishment of political supervision and shortly after the occupation of Nashville, Lincoln appointed Andrew Johnson military governor of Tennessee.

President Lincoln held that secession was impossible and that the so-called Confederacy was in a state of insurrection. He believed that it was his duty as chief executive to not only put down the insurrection but to restore loyal state governments in the South as quickly as possible. The president entrusted the responsibility for reestablishing loyal government in Tennessee to Andrew Johnson. Unfortunately, the military governor was unsuited to the task and his appointment was unwise. Born in North Carolina, Johnson moved to Greenville, Tennessee, as a young man and worked as a tailor. He became involved in politics as a Democrat and, according to legend, was the spokesman of small farmers. Johnson served five terms in the United States House of Representatives and two terms as governor. In 1857, he was elected to the United States Senate and was serving in that body when Tennessee seceded. Johnson, however, proclaimed his allegiance to the Union and remained at his Senate post, a stance that was applauded by Unionist Democrats. He was especially harsh in denouncing secession, planters, and the institution of slavery and this made him unpopular in the middle and western sections of the state. Whigs were incensed when Lincoln awarded control of federal patronage in Tennessee to the loyal Democratic senator. Andrew Johnson was energetic, hardworking, and forthright, but he was also arrogant, stubborn, and abrasive in dealing with people. He was therefore not suited for the role of peacemaking and reconciliation. The task before him would have strained the talents in the best of leaders.

Johnson's attempt to reconstruct Tennessee was an exercise in frustration as it proved virtually impossible to reconcile the various elements in the state. Many secessionists sincerely believed in the South's cause and the possibility that a Confederate army might deliver the state from Union occupation did not inspire Southern sympathizers to participate in restoring loyal government. As Peter Maslowski has suggested, some secessionists were reluctant to abandon the Confederacy because of their distrust of Johnson. The military governor also had trouble reconciling differences among unionists whose positions ranged from conservative to moderate to radical. Johnson also contributed to the problems of reconstruction by his own ineptness. He often quarreled with army field commanders. More important, he first pursued a moderate and conciliatory policy toward secessionists, a stance that angered radical unionists. When there was no rush from Confederate sympathizers to proclaim allegiance, the governor decided that "treason must be made odious" and began a policy of repression. Secessionists were disfranchised and denied civil rights. Officeholders who refused to take an oath of allegiance to the United States were summarily removed and some were jailed. The new policy may have pleased radicals but conservative and even some moderate unionists were alienated. Johnson's first attempt to restore the electoral process was anything but a rousing success. The governor authorized the holding of county election in March 1864 and decreed that all voters must take an oath of allegiance. Secessionists were already excluded but conservative unionists boycotted the elections. Many loyalists, especially in East Tennessee, humiliated by the oath requirement, refused to participate. The turnout was therefore low and disappointing.

Finally, in January 1865, as the war was drawing to a close and the Confederacy dying, a convention was held in Nashville to amend the state's fundamental law and restore loyal government in Tennessee. Because secessionists were disfranchised and conservative loyalists alienated, the convention was dominated by radical

Unionists, most of whom were former Whigs. The convention adopted amendments abolishing slavery, repudiating secession, and nullifying all acts of the Confederate state government and scheduled an election to select a legislature and a governor. The convention's actions were ratified in a referendum in February and on 4 March 1865, William Gannaway "Parson" Brownlow was elected to the governorship.

Meanwhile, Governor Johnson moved on to a position of greater responsibility. Elected Vice President in November 1864, he was sworn in on 4 March 1865 and assumed the presidency upon Lincoln's assassination the following month. Most observers, expecting Johnson to deal harshly with former Confederates, were shocked when he proclaimed a lenient policy of reconstruction. The presidential plan, as it was called, if permitted to stand, would have allowed the rebels to regain control of Southern state governments. Congress, however, rejected the president's plan and a period of bitter controversy ensued as the president and the national legislative body struggled over the process of reconstruction. Finally, a group known as Radical Republicans won control of Congress and, over Johnson's veto, enacted a series of measures known collectively as Congressional or Radical Reconstruction. The measures placed the Southern states under military occupation and set as prerequisites for readmission to the Union enfranchising of blacks and the ratification of the thirteenth amendment to the Constitution, which abolished slavery, and the fourteenth amendment, which guaranteed citizenship to former slaves.

Tennessee's experience during the Reconstruction era differed from other Southern states. In the first place the process started early in the war with military occupation and Johnson's military governorship. Moreover, the state was readmitted to the Union in July 1866, months before the Radicals in Congress enacted Congressional Reconstruction. Nevertheless, a homegrown brand of radicalism had already won control of the state and was allied with Radical Republicans in Washington. The years from 1865 to 1869 comprised a unique era in the Volunteer State. At no time before or since has a more extreme element controlled the political process in the state. The radical regime was able to dominate by following a policy of suppressing dissidents. The symbol of radicalism in Tennessee was Governor Brownlow.

A native of Virginia, William G. Brownlow was for a number of years an itinerant Methodist preacher and was known for his heated sermons. He turned to journalism in 1839, editing first the *Jonesboro Whig and Independent* and then the Knoxville *Whig*. He wrote with a caustic pen vilifying both political enemies and policies he opposed. A rabid unionist, Brownlow was vociferous in denouncing secession and during the war he developed a consummate hatred for secessionists. His dynamic and aggressive personality propelled him into the leadership of the radical unionists and thus the governor's office virtually unopposed in 1865. Brownlow formed the Radical Republican party in Tennessee and that party won control of the General Assembly in legislative elections in 1865. Brownlow had a pliant legislature and he ruled with an iron hand.

Brownlow was intent not only on suppressing the despised ex-Confederates but also in maintaining political control of the state. Every act of the governor and legislature in their first year of office was designed to achieve both goals. Acting upon Brownlow's recommendations, the General Assembly disfranchised secessionists and otherwise pursued a proscriptive and punitive policy regarding former Confederates. The state militia was strengthened ostensibly to be used against widespread guerrilla activity but it could also be used to intimidate political opponents. Also at Brownlow's urging, the legislature ratified the thirteenth amendment. The fourteenth amendment which was presented to the General Assembly in July 1866 proved troublesome to the radicals. Several conservatives were so opposed to the amendment that they absented themselves from the legislature to prevent a quorum. A quorum was achieved and thus ratification only after two representatives were arrested and taken to the legislative halls. Shortly after Tennessee's ratification of the fourteenth amendment, Congress passed a resolution restoring the state to the Union.

Since many of those disfranchised were Democrats, the party of Jefferson and Jackson was denied access to the political process and had no choice but to "lay low" for several years after the Civil War. Indeed, there was, for example, a reward for the arrest of Governor Harris and the fire-eating secessionist had to live in exile until the bounty was lifted in late 1867. The only effective opposition to the Brownlow regime came from conservatives of a Whiggish coloration. This element gave the governor cause for concern. Although he had supported slavery before the war and opposed enfranchising blacks, Brownlow was persuaded that he needed the votes of former slaves in order to survive. Therefore, in 1867, at the urging of the governor, the General Assembly gave blacks the franchise. Brownlow was also given extensive powers to regulate the voting process. In the elections later that year, the governor was re-elected overwhelmingly and the Radicals retained control of the legislature. The votes of former slaves were important in the outcome of the elections and no doubt black voting was a factor in an increase in the intimidation of former slaves and radicals by secret night-riding groups such as the Ku Klux Klan. Brownlow tried to suppress these activities but without measurable success. The vigilantes' violence and threats of violence may have contributed to the downfall of the radicals but the growing strength of the conservatives was more vital. The fall came when Brownlow was elected to the United States Senate.

Ambitious for national office, Governor Brownlow persuaded the legislature to elect him to the United States Senate to succeed David Patterson. Because the senatorial term began on 4 March 1869, Brownlow resigned the governorship in late February with less than a year remaining in his term. He was succeeded as governor by speaker of the State Senate DeWitt Clinton Senter. Brownlow had no reason to doubt Senter's loyalty to the radical cause for he had actively supported the former's proscriptive measures. When shortly the radicals met to nominate a gubernatorial candidate for the general election in late 1869, Senter put in his bid. Internal bickering split the radicals into two factions, one nominating Senter and the other, third district congressman William Brickly Stokes. The conservatives did not field a candidate but the race between Stokes and Senter was a bitter one. It appeared that the congressman had the support of a majority of the radicals. Therefore, in order to secure conservative votes, Senter lifted martial law and restored the franchise to secessionists. The move was decisive as Senter was elected by a sizable margin. Moreover, the conservatives won overwhelming control of the new General Assembly; the radicals retained only five seats in the Senate and seventeen in the House. The new legislature, determined to undo as much of Reconstruction as possible and wreak vengeance upon the hated radicals, repealed a number of measures enacted during the previous four years. The General Assembly also issued a call for a convention to rewrite the state's fundamental law, the voters approved, delegates were elected, and the convention convened in 1870.

The makeup of the constitutional convention of 1870 reflected not only the prevailing mood in Tennessee and the revulsion toward radicalism but also the political patterns that would evolve in the years that followed. Conspicuous by their absence were radical Republicans and fire-eating Democrats. There were no black delegates and only four Republicans were present. A few relatively moderate secessionist Democrats were in attendance but the extreme rebels, still in disrepute, had no representation. The working majority was conservative and made up largely of former Whigs with a variety of inclinations ranging from secessionist to unionist. They often quarreled among themselves over a variety of issues but they were of one mind in their desire to end the last vestiges of Radical Reconstruction in the state. This they proceeded to do with dispatch. Convinced that the legislature in the previous four years had levied excessive taxes and spent wastefully, the convention placed limitations on sources of revenue and established controls on spending. Restrictions were placed on the power of the governor and the amending process for the fundamental law was made difficult. The convention's only concession to radicalism was black voting. The majority of delegates probably preferred to disfranchise the former slave, but, perhaps out of fear of federal intervention, blacks were given the vote. However, the convention required that a poll tax be levied and that measure effectively eliminated the poor, both black and white, from the electoral process. The work of the convention complete, the new fundamental law was submitted to the voters in a referendum and was ratified by a wide margin. Thus Tennessee was redeemed from Radical Reconstruction and the redeemers were those with a Whiggish ancestry allied with conservative Democrats.

A good case can be made that events in Reconstruction in Tennessee had more to do with restructuring political party systems than did the Civil War. As a national organization, the Whig party had been dead for some years before the war and the new Republican party had appropriated the old economic and philosophical biases of Whiggery. There were proposals after the war to revive the party but the timid efforts in that direction proved futile. With restoration out of the question, the homeless former Whigs in the Volunteer State faced two undesirable alternatives. One was to go with the Grand Old Party and a number took that route. To many others the idea of joining the party that had imposed radical measures was repugnant. The other alternative was to become Democrats and, because the conservatism of the party of Jefferson and Jackson was more harmonious with their philosophical inclinations than Republicanism, many did so with a vengeance. Although some so detested the term Democrat that they merely referred to themselves as conservative, others made a concession and accepted Democratic and Conservative as the name of the party. Thus the Democracy, the party that emerged as the dominant party in Tennessee after Reconstruction, took on a heavy Whig coloration and the term conservative was soon dropped.

The dominant Democratic party was a congeries of disparate elements. In addition to an assortment of former Whigs, the party contained secessionist Democrats and unionist Democrats of the Andrew Johnson variety. By 1872, old fire-eaters began to emerge from exile. What held this unusual collection together was fear of a potential Republican victory in the state. The fear was well founded. Despite being tinged with radicalism, Republicans emerged from Reconstruction as a strong minority party that could win statewide races if the Democracy was split. There were small pockets of strength all over the state and a tier of counties bordering the Tennessee River in West Tennessee had Republican majorities. But it was in the eastern region of the state that the Grand Old Party was dominant. The Republican strength in that area cannot be explained simply because the section was Whig before the war, had few slaves, and was Union in sympathy. Although the Appalachian mountain people were not confronted by a large black voting population and the Civil War had eroded Southern sympathies, East Tennesseans generally objected to the radical Republican measures and opposed enfranchising blacks. Gordon McKinney suggests that local leaders shaped Republican policies to reflect the parochial interests of their constituents. In short, party bosses established Republicanism in East Tennessee. Whatever the reason for the Grand Old Party's dominance in the area, the party was strong enough across the state to be a constant threat to the hegemony of the Democracy. Democrats tended to vote Democratic out of fear of the party that was symbolic of the hated radicalism and Yankee challenges to the Southern "way of life," but Democratic unity during the redeemer era was tenuous.

One of the results of the new constitution was to change gubernatorial and legislative elections to even-numbered years. The first election was scheduled for November 1870. But in order to permit Governor Senter to complete a full term, the first governor elected under the new fundamental law would not assume office until October 1871 and would therefore serve a shortened term. Full two-year terms began in January 1873. As its candidate for governor in 1870, the conservative Democracy chose John Calvin Brown, brother of prewar Governor Neill Smith Brown. A former Whig, Brown had opposed secession but accepted it and served in the Confederate army, ultimately reaching the rank of general. In the general election, he easily defeated the Republican candidate, William Wisener of Shelbyville, by a two to one margin. The Democrats also retained control of the legislature. As governor, Brown demonstrated sympathy for railroad interests and pursued a policy of encouraging the consolidation of small lines. After leaving the governorship, Brown became a railroad executive and directed the construction of the Texas and Pacific Railway. He was for a short time president of the Tennessee Coal, Iron and Railway Company.

The semblance of unity in the Democracy was disrupted in 1872 when Andrew Johnson attempted a comeback. As a result of the census of 1870, Tennessee was awarded an additional congressional seat. Lacking time to carve out a new district, the legislature set the state as an at-large district. After failing to obtain the Democratic nomination for the new post in Congress, Johnson, who still had a sizable following, entered the race as an independent. Johnson drew enough votes away from the Democratic candidate so that the Republican, Horace Maynard, an outspoken radical, won the seat. In the same election, Governor Brown beat back a Republican attempt to unseat him. However, a number of Johnson's followers won legislative posts and, in alliance with other dissidents, gained control of the General Assembly in 1873. Even so, the Whiggish element held firm in the Democratic convention in 1874 to secure the gubernatorial nomination for James David Porter. A prewar Whig who saw service in the Confederate army, Porter defeated the Republican nominee with relative ease. After his two terms as governor, Porter became president of the Nashville, Chattanooga, and St. Louis Railroad. Despite the monopoly on the governor's office, the Whiggish element was unable to dominate the redeemer coalition. They lacked unity themselves and they were forced to make concessions to other powerful groups within the Democratic party.

In 1875, the old Jacksonian Democrat, Andrew Johnson, attempted another comeback and campaigned aggressively to win support for the United States Senate seat of retiring William G. Brownlow. The former President had bitter enemies but he also had a significant following. Two other candidates for the Senate placed their names before the General Assembly when it convened in January 1875: former governor Brown and the popular ex-Confederate general, William Brimage Bate. After a protracted struggle and fifty-five ballots, Johnson won the election. He died soon after assuming his position, however, which provided the General Assembly of 1877 with the opportunity to fill both Senate posts at the same time. An old Whig, James Edmund Bailey, was awarded Johnson's unexpired term after a difficult struggle. Then, surprisingly, Isham G. Harris was elected unanimously to a full term in the Senate. The victory of the latter indicated that the old fire-eating secessionists were no longer in disrepute. The old Whigs had never been in a commanding position and the state debt controversy further weakened their power and in fact brought about the breakup of the redeemer coalition.

The Tennessee state debt, amounting to almost forty million dollars in 1870, had been incurred both before the Civil War and during Brownlow's administration largely to assist private enterprise in building railroads. In 1873, at the behest of Governor Brown, the General Assembly funded the debt by issuing new bonds

carrying six percent interest. Later that same year, a severe economic depression set in and two years later, Tennessee defaulted
in interest payments. Hard times caused resentment among the
masses at paying taxes that would line the pockets of rich bondholders. Moreover, there was a widespread belief that had some validity that the proceeds of the bonds sold under the radical regime
had gone into the hands of corruptionists. The state debt thus became an emotionally volatile issue. Views on the debt ranged from
state creditors, those who advocated maintaining the state's credit
at full face value, to low taxers, those who urged that the debt be
scaled down or repudiated altogether. The low tax revolt gained
such momentum that, by 1878, full faith and credit was no longer
considered; the question became how much the debt would be
scaled back. The chief concern of the state creditors now was to
minimize the loss to the bondholders.

Although there were numerous exceptions, state creditors generally were former Whigs. They tended to take the position that the
state must assume its obligation to pay the debt at face value and
any suggestion to scale down the debt was morally indefensible.
They were therefore open to the charge that they supported an unfair burden on the taxpayers of Tennessee. Governor Brown, for
example, had endorsed the funding act of 1873, a measure favorable to bondholders. His successor, Governor Porter, insisted that
any scaling of the debt must receive prior approval of the bondholders. The position on the state debt taken by Brown and Porter
was an important factor in the fall from grace of the Whiggish element.

The state debt was the chief issue in the gubernatorial contest
in 1878 and when the Democrats met in convention to nominate a
candidate, the battle was on. There were five contenders including
Governor Porter representing state creditors and varying degrees
on the low-tax scale. The first day's balloting was indecisive but on
the second day, someone placed the name of Judge Albert Smith
Marks of Franklin County in nomination. A contrived bandwagon
began to roll and Marks won the nomination. The factions coalesced behind Marks and he won the governorship in the general
election. Although a unionist Democrat, Marks served in the Confederate army and rose to the rank of colonel before losing a leg in

the battle of Murfreesboro. An indecisive man, the new governor
was too cautious to provide the leadership to solve the debt controversy. Pursuing an ambiguous course, Marks merely recom-
mended settlement of the problem. A quarreling General Assembly
in 1879 therefore scaled down the debt by fifty percent at four percent interest, pursuant to the approval of the voters in a referendum. In a low turnout, the electorate rejected the fifty-to-one
settlement by a significant margin. The controversy was still un-
settled and by 1880, the Democratic party was clearly divided over
the issue.

When the Democracy met in convention in 1880 to nominate a
candidate for the governor's race, the cleavage became complete
when low taxers bolted leaving state creditors in control of the pro-
ceedings. Normally incumbent chief executives were rewarded with
a second nomination, but the rump state creditors nominated John
Vines Wright of Columbia, who advocated a settlement that would
be "fair" to the bondholders. The low taxers nominated Samuel
Franklin Wilson of Sumner County. The Democratic split gave
hopes to the Republicans who nominated a state creditor, Alvin
Hawkins from Huntingdon in Carroll County. Wilson came in third
but he took enough votes away from Wright to give the election to
Hawkins by a plurality in the general election. In the legislative session in 1881, an alliance of state credit Republicans and Democrats
funded the debt at face value at three percent interest. Low taxers
were indignant but the State Supreme Court shortly voided the
measure. Hawkins then called the legislature into extraordinary
session but the General Assembly was unable to effect a solution to
the debt controversy during his term. In the senatorial contest in
1881, a majority of Republicans, unable to elect their favorite son,
united with the supporters of state representative Howell Ed-
munds Jackson of Jackson in Madison County, to unseat the incumbent, James E. Bailey and send Jackson to the United States
Senate.

Sobered by the split that had resulted in the election of a Republican governor, Democrats began to move toward unity. The
leader of this movement was Senator Harris, who took a centrist
position and, urging compromise, successfully wooed low taxers
back into the fold. Indeed, the low taxers dominated the guber-

natorial nomination convention in 1882 and drafted a plank that
called for scaling the debt by fifty percent at three percent interest.
There were six contenders for the nomination but the strongest was
the old fire-eater and Confederate general, William B. Bate, who
received the nod on the fifth ballot. A few last-ditch state creditors,
known as "sky blues," and led by Duncan Brown Cooper bolted the
convention but they exercised little influence in the subsequent
campaign. Harmony prevailed in the Democratic party and Bate
easily defeated Governor Hawkins in the general election. Bate's
victory signaled the end of the state debt controversy. The depression of the 1870s was over, prosperity had returned, and the public
seemed to be tired of the issue. The General Assembly of 1883
moved to end the problem of the debt permanently. A funding
measure, similar to the one defeated in the referendum four years
earlier, scaled the debt to fifty percent of face value at three percent interest. The issue was thus buried.

More important than the settling of the controversy, Bate's
election was the beginning of a new era in Tennessee politics. The
state credit stance of the old Whig redeemers discredited that element and a new coalition moved to fill the vacuum. Secessionist
Democrats, demonstrating a willingness to adjust and adapt to
changing conditions and led by Senator Harris, appropriated the
center, and gained dominance of the Democratic party. This coalition became known as the Bourbon "regulars."

Chapter 2

Bourbons
and Populists

Historians are wont to classifying, synthesizing, generalizing, and interpreting the phenomena of the past. A case in point is the scholarly attempt to explain Democratic divisiveness in Tennessee in the post-Reconstruction era. Thus Daniel Merritt Robison early identified three factions: states'-rights planters, Whig industrialists, and small farmers. According to Robison's stereotypes, the states'-rights planters were latter-day Bourbons who were conservative if not mossback reactionaries. The Whig industrialists were the Redeemer advocates of a New South, a creed that encouraged economic development in Tennessee through greater capital investment to tap natural resources, improve transportation, and in general promote industrialization. The small farmers were supporters of Andrew Johnson and traced their ancestry back to the "common man" of Andrew Jackson's day.

More recently, Roger L. Hart, after carefully examining Tennessee in the generation after Reconstruction, challenged Robison's simplistic view. Hart argues that "differences within the dominant Democratic party did not give rise to continuing, organized, and clearly defined factions." Hart concluded that the various groups identified by Robison "were not disciplined, cohesive factions, but loose coalitions based more on patronage and sym-

bolic issues than on conflicts among sections or classes with different economic interests." Making it more difficult to place Democrats
into neat categories was the fact that local, county, and regional
leaders did not always fit factional stereotypes. Successful politicians were pragmatic; often the highest bid or promises of patronage were more important to local leaders than adherence to abstract
principles. Moreover, what V. O. Key, Jr. called the "friends and
neighbors vote," that is, casting ballots for a local favorite son,
sometimes violated factional lines. Despite the confusing nature of
Tennessee's Democratic party, there was an element of truth in
Robison's categories, as there is in all stereotypes. Small farmers
achieved a measure of cohesiveness in the early 1890s. The terms
Whig industrialist and Bourbon are useful in making distinctions
among the various political and economic persuasions and philosophical biases of individuals and groups.

   Whig industrialists did indeed endorse the New South creed.
There was a tendency for Whig industrialists to be sympathetic to
railroads and to advocate a high tariff to protect domestic industry
and other forms of assistance for economic enterprise. They also
tended to oppose state regulation of business, particularly railroads. Because they believed that a good educational system would
help attract industry, Whig industrialists were willing to accept federal aid for schools in Tennessee. The term Bourbon is a bit more
elusive and a few modern scholars reject it as too imprecise for definition. The expression was first used by contemporaries in the post-
Reconstruction period to identify old states'-rights planter aristo-
crats and mossback reactionaries who were always looking back-
wards and allegedly learned nothing and forgot nothing. Later
observers accepted the stereotype and also identified the Bourbons
with the romantic cult of the Old South. While conceding the am-
biguities of the term, most modern Southern historians find it useful in identifying a broadly based community of interests. Bourbons
cannot be fitted into a neat stereotype, but certain generalizations
can be made.

   Bourbons, in the tradition of the old planters and other agrarian interests, opposed tariff protection and state aid to economic
enterprise. Many indeed favored regulation of business. Recalling
the hated measures and federal actions during Radical Reconstruc-

tion, Bourbons were bitterly opposed to threats of Yankee intervention in the internal affairs of the state. They were especially hostile to proposals to enforce black voting and congressional appropriations for education in Tennessee. Certainly the ranks included reactionaries and unreconstructed rebels, but most Bourbons accepted progress and were advocates of the New South creed. They became businessmen with a vengeance and they could be found in the corporate boardrooms and even as managers of railroads. Their views on the tariff, regulation, and state subsidies to business varied with their economic interests. Tennessee's Bourbons spoke the rhetoric of progress and in so doing helped to create the myth that a new, prosperous, and industrialized South had in fact been achieved. At the same time they preserved the romantic image of the Old South, portraying it as a veritable utopia. They also glorified the Lost Cause, thus making it a symbol of nationalism and patriotism. As George Brown Tindall observed, they "kept alive the vision of an organic community with its personal relationships, its class distinctions, its habits of deference to the squirearchy." Bourbons spoke the words of progress and indeed made some commitment to innovation, but their chief concern was to the principles of states' rights, laissez-faire, and white supremacy. The differences between Bourbons and Whig industrialists on economic and symbolic issues were therefore only a matter of degree. Politically, the Bourbon element became a vested interest known as the "regulars" and was the conservative coalition within Tennessee's Democratic party.

The election of an old fire-eating Democrat to the governorship in 1882, William B. Bate, brought to an end the control of the Democracy by the Whig Redeemers and was the beginning of an era of dominance by the Bourbon regulars. The Bourbons had been able to beat back the Whig industrialists by adopting the rubric of reform and by espousing the New South creed. Although substantive, symbolic, and philosophical issues were important, once in power, the chief concern of the regulars became maintaining political control. This was evident in the career of Senator Isham G. Harris, the leader of the regulars. Harris had been a fire-eating secessionist and his star had been in eclipse during Reconstruction. Adjusting to the times, he became a Redeemer and was rewarded with election to the Senate in 1877. In 1882, Harris seized the initiative and brought a measure of unity in the Democratic party over the debt issue. From that point until his death in 1877, he was the dominant political leader in Tennessee. Harris had little interest in business or industry; rather, he was a consummate, pragmatic politician, capable of temporizing and compromising to maintain his political leadership. He, along with other Bourbon regulars, won a monopoly in the power structure in the state after 1882 and, as with any vested interest, sought to maintain the status quo. The regulars therefore stressed party unity and harmony and tried to suppress any issue or movement that threatened their hegemony. Especially did they emphasize the threat from the Republican party. Yankees with proposals to change the Southern way of life became convenient bugbears to distract public attention from internal conflict. But like the Redeemers, the Bourbon regulars were unable to create a disciplined, homogeneous party. Not only were they frequently challenged by other elements in the party, the regulars often quarreled among themselves. The lack of cohesiveness among the Bourbons was evident on the issue of railroad regulation.

There were legitimate grievances against the transportation monopoly, the railroads. Abuses included favoritism, kickbacks, and discrimination in freight rates. By the 1880s, the demands for regulation and reform of railroads reached significant proportions and the Bourbon regulars tried to exploit the issue. When the General Assembly met in 1883, the regulars sponsored a measure that would create a regulatory commission. Railroad lobbyists and Whiggish Democrats such as former governors Brown and Porter mobilized the opposition and the bill that passed established a weak and ineffective agency. Two years later, the legislature abolished the railroad commission. The Bourbons had clearly been unable to hold all of the regulars in line for regulation. On the other hand, Whiggish Democrats were unable to coalesce behind a challenger, whereas Bourbon lines held firm and Bate won renomination in the Democratic convention in 1884. The Republicans put up Frank T. Reid, a former Whig and a member of a prominent Nashville family. In the campaign, Reid denounced the debt settlement as morally indefensible. Many Whiggish Democrats, unhappy over the settlement, defected to Reid and Bate barely won reelection. His margin of victory was only about seven thousand votes and three percent of the total. The regulars achieved a measure of discipline two years later. Although it took some sixty-eight ballots in the Democratic caucus in 1887, Bourbon lines held firm and Governor Bate won nomination and was subsequently elected to the United States Senate by the General Assembly, replacing Howell Jackson. Bate's opponents had been unable to hold together. Thus the Bourbon coalition monopolized both Senate posts and the occupants were former fire-eating secessionists. Yet because of internal disorganization and conflicting personal ambitions, the regulars lost the governorship in 1886.

Indicative of the weakness of the Bourbon regulars was their inability to agree on a candidate for governor in 1886. When the Democrats assembled in convention, the field was crowded but dwindled to four leading aspirants. Sectional antagonism limited the attraction of most. Only Robert Love Taylor, a youthful East Tennessee Democrat had statewide appeal. A one-term congressman, Taylor had been a strong rival for James E. Bailey's Senate seat in 1881 and he was a contender for the gubernatorial nomination in 1882. After fifteen ballots, Taylor's managers succeeded in winning nomination for the popular independent Democrat. In the name of unity and fear of a Republican victory, the regulars reluctantly endorsed Taylor. Perhaps they hoped to absorb him into the regular coalition. The threat of a Republican victory in the gubernatorial election was real. The Grand Old Party countered by nominating Taylor's brother, Alfred Alexander Taylor, and the resultant campaign became the legendary "war of the roses." The brothers were from a prominent family in the northeastern corner of the state. Their father, Nathaniel Greene Taylor, had been a Whig unionist congressman and other members of the family had served in positions of political responsibility. The family divided its sympathies during the Civil War, and afterwards Bob became a Democrat and Alf a Republican. The canvass proved to be a festive affair with more style than substance as the brothers toured the state debating each other and delighting appreciative audiences by playing the fiddle. Robert Taylor, "Our Bob" as he was affectionately known, was more entertainer than politician. A good speaker, he amused audiences with droll, humorous stories while successfully evading issues. Indeed, his funny stories attracted attention while his ambiguous pronouncements and empty banalities on the questions of the day left his listeners uncertain as to his beliefs. Nevertheless, he was, in 1886, well on the way to becoming one of the state's most popular political leaders. His victory margin in the governor's race, however, was narrow. He polled some 16,000 more votes than Alf. While significantly better than Bate's majority in 1884, Bob Taylor's victory was largely the result of the Democratic voting habit in Tennessee. The important point is that Bourbon regulars had lost the governor's office. The status among the factions of the new governor has been a matter in dispute among historians.

Dan Robison concluded that Bob Taylor, in the tradition of Jackson and Johnson, was the leader of the small farmers in Tennessee's Democracy. Moreover, he kept discontented farmers in the party and prevented the later agrarian protest movement from taking a radical turn. Roger Hart has challenged the Robison thesis, insisting that Taylor was not the small-farmer candidate; rather, he was Whiggish in inclination and an advocate of the New South creed. Hart presents a convincing argument. Taylor's chief backers, for example, were New South advocates such as industrialist and journalist Arthur St. Clair Colyar. His policies also revealed a touch of Whiggery. Hart might have added that no one glorified the romantic myth of the Old South more than Taylor while expounding on the New South creed. No one in his generation reconciled tradition with innovation more than "Our Bob."

Taylor revealed his sympathies soon after he became governor in January 1887 when he awarded patronage to Whiggish New South men. Then in a message to the legislature in February, Governor Taylor urged support for the Blair bill. A measure then pending in Congress, the Blair bill proposed to distribute federal funds to the states for educational purposes. Although Tennessee would have received a sizable amount of money under the act, Bourbons regarded it as an invasion of states' rights and just another attempt by Northern Republicans to meddle in the internal affairs of the states. During the gubernatorial campaign, Taylor had been closely watched by the regulars for a commitment on the bill, but the candidate successfully evaded the issue. The Bourbons were therefore incredulous when Taylor endorsed the Blair proposal. Newspaper editors of the Bourbon persuasion denounced the governor for this treason to the South and to the Democratic party. Taylor further alienated the regulars for his opposition to railroad regulation. Thoroughly unhappy with the governor's record, the Bourbons made a concerted effort to deny him renomination in 1888. When the Democratic nomination convention met, the regulars controlled a majority of delegates but they were unable to agree among themselves on a candidate. Taylor, however, held his delegates in line and after a bitter struggle and forty ballots, he received the party's nod. He won reelection in part because Democrats feared that a split would open the door for a Republican victory.

Despite internal bickering, the Democracy achieved near unanimity in the passage of a series of election reforms enacted by the General Assembly in 1889 and 1890. One measure instituted the secret ballot in the larger communities. The act provided for an indirect literacy test, for it prohibited giving assistance in casting a ballot to anyone unable to read. A second bill called for voter registration in the cities. Another act, designed to preclude federal interference in state elections, provided for separate ballot boxes for federal and state elections. Finally, because the first had been repealed, the legislature carried out the constitutional mandate by imposing a poll tax on the franchise. The net effect of these measures was to reduce the vote of the poor and illiterate, and especially blacks, and because most Negroes cast Republican ballots, the vote for that party was reduced significantly.

Some scholars hold that the election laws were not racially motivated. Roger Hart, however, insists that the goal of white supremacy was an important factor behind passage of the measures and produces abundant evidence to confirm his contention. Joseph H. Cartwright demonstrates that initially, Bourbons were paternalistic toward blacks and, in an effort to broaden their base of support, actively courted black votes. Before the end of the 1880s, however, the regulars had become disillusioned and, with the cooperation of Whiggish New South men and some Republicans, "determined to crush black political influence." Democratic newspapers were the vanguard in the campaign. Editors fulminated against black suffrage. Negroes, they claimed, were, as a whole, ignorant and easily corrupted. The electoral process could therefore be purified by eliminating the mass of venal voters. These editors were not reluctant to point out that blacks tended to vote the Republican ticket and for the party that had imposed radicalism on the South and regularly proposed measures that involved violations of the rights of the states. Tennessee did not, of course, follow the pattern of the deep South by mass disfranchisement by statute. Blacks could still vote in the Volunteer State and in fact urban bosses found their ballots useful, but suffrage for this minority was reduced and under greater control. Thus with the Bourbons taking the initiative, white supremacy was established and, as Cartwright demonstrates, "Jim Crow" triumphed in Tennessee. The victors had the cooperation of Governor Taylor.

Despite having alienated many Bourbons, Taylor left the governor's office in 1891 a relatively popular political leader. Because he was ambitious and had his eye on a seat in the United States Senate, Taylor had neither pressed progressive measures very hard nor redirected the course of the Democracy in Tennessee. Likewise he could not prevent nor did he have the power to control the agrarian revolt that burst upon the Volunteer State in 1890 with surprising suddenness. This small-farmer movement contained a much greater threat to Bourbon hegemony than Robert L. Taylor.

The agrarian revolt was a mass movement that erupted across the South and West in 1890. For more than a generation, small farmers had been plagued by declining market prices for farm products while the exactions of middlemen, interest rates, freight rates, and taxes remained high. The root of the farmers' problems, however, was the declining status of the time-honored yeoman farmer while the political power of urban and industrial America increased. Nevertheless, the farmers placed the blame for their plight on corporate monopolies and railroad interests, urban political machines, and their alleged sycophants in political office. Small farmers therefore began to organize in an effort to obtain relief and by 1890, with a variety of economic and political proposals designed to curb or regulate business interests, the movement had blossomed into a full-scale revolt against the political establishment.

The agrarian revolt originated in Tennessee, as elsewhere, with fraternal organizations. In the late 1880s two small farmer brotherhoods merged under the banner of the Farmers' Alliance. Although originally nonpolitical, under the leadership of men of experience and prominence in the small towns of the state, the fraternal order turned to political action. The political establishment in the Volunteer State was not unaware of the rumblings of discontent in the rural areas but did not regard the Alliance as a genuine threat even though the General Assembly of 1889 contained a number of Alliance men. Indeed, the Bourbons shared many of the small farmers' grievances. Both groups, for example, favored tariff reduction, business regulation, and currency inflation. The regulars merely patronized the farmers by reminding them that they could obtain relief only through the Democratic party.

As if to take them at their word, the upstart farmer organization stunned the complacent Bourbons by seizing control of the Democratic party and the governorship in 1890. Prior to the Democratic nominating convention, there were several hopefuls but only three emerged as serious contenders: Josiah Patterson, a Bourbon stalwart from Memphis, Jere Baxter, a New South man and Nashville railroad executive, and John Price Buchanan of Rutherford County, president of the state Alliance. Buchanan was not regarded seriously until a grass-roots boom in the rural areas developed, and he went to the convention with commitments from almost half the delegates. It took more than two dozen ballots but Buchanan won the nomination largely because of antagonism between the Patterson and Baxter camps and their unwillingness to compromise. Many Democratic factions were unhappy with the nominee and they were sorely tempted to bolt the party or remain inactive in the campaign. Fear of a Republican victory, especially after the GOP convention endorsed the Lodge Force bill, a measure before Congress that would require federal supervision of elections in the South, no doubt encouraged many Democrats to remain loyal. Buchanan won by a good majority and a significant number of Alliance men were elected to the legislature.

The Tennessee Farmers' Alliance was therefore in a commanding position in politics after the election of 1890. The organization, however, provides an interesting study in contradictions. The Al-

liance in the Volunteer State did not fit the stereotype of an organization of "hayseed socialists" or rustic radicals. While the
membership did indeed include poor farmers, the rolls of the organization included a goodly number of large landowners and the
leaders were certainly not radicals. As Roger Hart has docu-
mented, men of some wealth, prominence, and political experience in the small towns of the state constituted the leadership both
in local chapters and in the hierarchy of the state Alliance. Governor Buchanan, for example, was hardly a poor farmer. He owned
a farm of more than three hundred acres, had long been politically
active in his county, and had served in the General Assembly four
years before becoming the state's chief executive. Those who made
policy and directed the course of the farmer organization were men
of ambition. With the internal paths to positions of responsibility
choked by vested interests, these men seized the Alliance as a ve-
hicle to gain power and prestige. The membership and leadership
of the farmer organization in Tennessee thus did not constitute a
collection of fanatics pressing extreme measures. The state group,
for example, hesitated to endorse a proposal of the national Alliance that called for federal loans to farmers for nonperishable crops.
The program, known as the Subtreasury Plan, was bitterly opposed by conservatives. The Democratic platform of 1890 did, at
the urging of Alliance men, contain a plank supporting currency
inflation by free coinage of silver but Tennessee's Bourbons had no
reason to oppose the proposition. Finally, contrary to the long-held
interpretation, the Alliance in the state did not develop an early association with blacks. Rather, the white organization was paternalistic toward the Colored Alliance and Alliance men in the legislature
supported the disfranchising measures of 1889 and 1890. Clearly,
the Alliance constituted no threat to the established social order in
Tennessee.

     The nature of the agrarian revolt in Tennessee was revealed in
the policies and practices of the Buchanan administration. A number of the governor's appointments and a good deal of patronage
went to conservatives and Buchanan presented no social reforms
for the legislature to consider. The Alliance men in the General Assembly were primarily conservative Democrats. There was no inclination among them to pursue radical or even moderately

progressive measures. The Alliance had achieved a commanding position in Tennessee without a set of goals or a program. The leaders often disagreed among themselves over issues such as railroad regulation. The farmers' organization did not even have a caucus in the legislature. It is clear that the Alliance leadership, if not the membership as a whole, was conservative and had no intention of promoting social change. Yet the established factions regarded the upstart farmers as a threat but not for radicalism. The ascendancy of the Alliance was viewed as a genuine threat to the Democracy in Tennessee.

The rise to power of the Farmers' Alliance had upset the political status quo in the Volunteer State. But to both Bourbons and New South men alike, the concern was less with extreme measures than with political control. The farmer organization had the potential for wrecking the Democratic party in Tennessee and ominous events beyond the state seemed to confirm the fears of the established factions. The national Farmers' Alliance with other dissident groups began a movement toward a new political party that would be more responsive than the two major parties to the demands of farmers and laborers. After a series of meetings over a number of months, a convention composed of the leaders of the Alliance, organized labor, and the old Greenback party met in Cincinnati, Ohio, in May 1891 and adopted a resolution supporting the formation of a third party. Then at St. Louis, Missouri, the following February, the People's party or Populist party, as it was called, was formally organized. The Populists met again in July 1892, nominated a candidate for the presidency, and presented a long list of demands that included currency expansion by the free and unlimited coinage of silver, political and economic reforms, business regulation, and federally sponsored programs to aid farmers. Growing increasingly alarmed as these events unfolded, the political establishment in Tennessee determined to crush the Alliance in the state and deny Buchanan renomination in 1892. Bourbons and New South men, in an unprecedented show of unity, joined hands in a massive and vicious propaganda campaign to end political control of the Volunteer State by the upstart farmer organization.

The Farmers' Alliance of Tennessee refused to give a blanket endorsement to the national organization's proposed reforms and tried to disassociate itself from the third-party movement. Like other Southern Alliance men, Tennesseans were reluctant to give up allegiance to the Democratic party. Yet, because they were a part of the national organization, the state group shared the stigma of radicalism. With no little exaggeration, their opponents lost no time in exploiting the stigma and pronounced the state Alliance guilty by association. By the summer of 1891, editorials denouncing the organization became a regular feature in newspapers of both Bourbon and New South persuasion. According to the editorials, Alliance leaders were fanatics supporting programs that would bring about social upheaval if not wreck and ruin to the nation. White Alliance leaders were charged with having a close, intimate relationship with Colored Alliance men and that one of the goals of the organization was social equality for blacks. Editors made it clear that they were not opposed to small farmers and they conceded that the agrarians had legitimate complaints. Emphasizing loyalty to the Democracy, small farmers were told that they could gain relief only through that party. The effectiveness of the propaganda campaign cannot be measured but clearly something more was needed to discredit the Alliance and Buchanan. John Henry McDowell, Buchanan's successor as president of the state Alliance was an attractive target for a scandal.

A native of West Tennessee, McDowell had served in the Confederate army and had lived in Arkansas for several years after the war. Returning to his native state, he rose in politics, became a recruiter for the Alliance, and was editor of the farmer organization's *Weekly Toiler* before assuming the state presidency. An associate and ally of Buchanan, the arrogant, vain, and ambitious McDowell was the ideal person to be singled out for attack. In June 1891, one of the state's leading newspapers in a flamboyant manner produced an "exposé" of McDowell's activities while a resident in Arkansas. He was accused of being a Republican officeholder and socially intimate with blacks. Whether the charges were true or false or merely exaggerated was immaterial. Virtually every daily newspaper in the state seized the allegations and, in Machiavellian style, regularly repeated them until few doubted their validity. The attacks on

McDowell indirectly embarrassed and damaged politically his ally Governor Buchanan. The governor was also hurt by his handling of a violent coal miners' strike in East Tennessee.

By the spring of 1892, the campaign against Buchanan had reached steamroller proportions. Bourbon and New South men had coalesced behind state Supreme Court Justice Peter Turney of Winchester as a candidate for the Democratic gubernatorial nomination. A Bourbon, Turney's earliest claim to fame was as an impatient secessionist. Annoyed at the reluctance of Tennessee to join the Confederacy, he led a movement for his native Franklin County to secede and become part of Alabama. As the boom for Turney developed, Buchanan's fortunes declined. In May, the Populist party was formally organized in Tennessee. Although Alliance leaders played no part in the formation of the party, Buchanan and Alliance Democrats were placed in a difficult position. The threat of a third party and the possibility that the governor would go with it caused many Alliance men to go over to Turney. Seeing the inevitable, Buchanan withdrew from the race and Turney became the Democratic gubernatorial nominee without opposition. The governor, however, did not disappear. He announced as an independent candidate for reelection, and was subsequently endorsed by the Populists. Thus, with a Republican candidate in the field, the gubernatorial contest became a three-way race.

The canvass of 1892 was an unusually shrill one. Democrats insisted that the Populist party was a threat to the racial mores of the state because of a commitment to social equality for blacks. Although most Populists were hostile to race mixing and denied the charge, the point was telling and the threat to white supremacy undoubtedly caused many Democrats to remain loyal. More important in the outcome of the election was an alliance between Populists and Republicans. The two parties quietly agreed to avoid certain congressional and legislative races in hopes of increasing the number of Populists and Republicans elected. The deal, when exposed by the Democratic press, probably encouraged many undecided and lukewarm Populists to vote with the Democracy. Turney won the governor's office by a healthy plurality; Buchanan ran a poor third. The Alliance also lost heavily in the legislative races. Thus the

Bourbons once again controlled the political machinery in the state and the Alliance threat had been beaten back.

The election of 1892 signaled the end of the political influence of the Farmers' Alliance in Tennessee. A number of factors contributed to the fall of the farmer organization. The Alliance rose to power with no goals and no positive program. Its leaders were inept if not incompetent and as conservative as the Bourbons. What the agrarian revolt in Tennessee lacked was a charismatic leader who could rally discontent to bring about political and economic reforms. A good case can be made that the truly disaffected in the Volunteer State constituted a relatively small minority and that the most dynamic leader would have had difficulty in achieving social change in the face of strenuous opposition of the conservative majority that could be found in both the Democratic and Republican parties. In any case, the Bourbons, assisted by Whiggish New South men, portrayed the Alliance and the Populists as threats to the existing values, norms, and beliefs. The upstart farmer organization was thus crushed and, in retrospect, it appears to have been accomplished with relative ease. In a real sense, the Alliance day in the sun in Tennessee was an aberration.

With Senator Bate's reelection in early 1893, Isham G. Harris occupying the other Senate post, and Turney in the governor's office, the Bourbon coalition once again controlled all the major state offices for the first time in six years. Bourbons were also in a strong position in the legislature, but the renewed conservative hegemony was tenuous. The Republican party was still a strong minority and the organized Populist party contained a number of dissidents. Moreover, the grievances of small farmers, whether real, imaginary, or simply a matter of status anxiety, had not been addressed. Distress in the countryside was exacerbated by the onset of a severe economic depression in 1893. The conservative nature of the regular coalition precluded aggressive action on social problems and the Bourbons were especially careful not to muddy the waters. Rather than discussing issues, the Bourbons emphasized harmony and regularity in their propaganda. The leaders insisted that the only way to meet the menace of Populism and other threats to social stability was for the rank and file to remain loyal to the Democratic party.

Despite its shaky control of the political machinery in Tennessee, the regulars seemingly became complacent and there was some justification for this. The Populist party was not a healthy organization and its leaders quarreled among themselves. There was also bitter conflict within the Republican party between the "native whites" and the newcomers or "carpetbaggers." So confident were the regulars that they renominated Turney unanimously for the governorship in 1894 despite the fact that he had been unable to generate enthusiasm among the electorate. The Populists put up a candidate and the Republicans nominated a "carpetbagger," Henry Clay Evans, a Chattanooga industrialist originally from Pennsylvania. The outcome of the hard-fought race stunned the overconfident Democrats. Evans won by a plurality and a razor-thin edge over Turney. Although the Populist candidate polled only ten percent of the vote, it was easily the difference in the outcome of the election. Unfortunately for the Republicans, the Democrats were unwilling to concede defeat and had an advantage: control of the legislature. When the General Assembly met in January 1895, a contested elections measure was enacted and a committee was appointed to investigate voting irregularities in the gubernatorial election. Ignoring fraud in Democratic districts, the committee found evidence in numerous cases in Republican East Tennessee where voters had not paid the poll tax. Those ballots were thrown out and Turney was certified the winner. Thus by an unfair method, Evans was denied his rightful victory and the Bourbon regulars were assured control of the governor's office for two more years. Nevertheless, the narrow escape forced the conservative coalition to reappraise the Democracy's position on the crucial and emotional issues of the day. One thing seemed clear: the party's policies were not responsive to the demands for change. The Bourbon regulars therefore boarded the reform bandwagon with a vengeance and seized the most convenient and, to conservatives, the most compatible issue, currency reform.

The money supply in the United States had long been a controversial issue. Generally, Eastern banking and business interests—creditors—favored a stable or hard currency, gold. Southern and Western agrarian interests—debtors—advocated inflating the money supply in the belief that the market price of staple crops would increase as a result and also make it easier to meet debt obligations. One group, the Greenbackers, advocated the use of fiat money to expand the currency supply. A stronger movement proposed the use of silver as a means of inflation. In 1878, Congress provided for a nominal amount of silver and the Sherman Act of 1890 increased that figure significantly. Even so, the per capita amount of money in circulation continued to decline. The Alliance claimed that the hard money policy was the cause of the farmers' economic plight and the free and unlimited coinage of silver to inflate the currency became one of the chief demands of the Populist party. But in 1893, after a gold panic and the onset of depression, President Grover Cleveland sought a solution to economic distress by forcing through Congress repeal of the Sherman Act. The President's efforts to return to one standard, gold, caused a bitter split in the national Democratic party between hard money Easterners and the inflationist South and West. The latter literally stole the Populist free silver demand and ran away with it. Democrats in the Volunteer State experienced a similar split.

In search of an issue after the scare in the election of 1894, Tennessee's Bourbon regulars found it easy to swim with the tide. Free and unlimited coinage of silver was the most easily acceptable of the Populists' goals, for Bourbons had long tended to favor an inflationist policy, but the zeal with which they seized and exploited the issue more than matched the Populists in the state. Even the pragmatic Senator Harris, after testing the waters, made a commitment to the white metal. But the regulars' enthusiasm for silver caused a split in the party much like the one over the state debt. Like the state creditors, Whiggish New South men tended to be gold bugs. Although the lines of similarity were not exact, the conflict between the advocates of hard money and the silverites was as intense as the conflict over the state debt.

The political contests in 1896 in Tennessee were therefore bitter and confusing. There were two hard-fought congressional races between hard money advocates and silverites with the latter winning. Populists were thrown into chaos when the Democratic party selected William Jennings Bryan as presidential candidate on a free silver platform. The national Populists had little choice but to endorse Bryan and Tennessee Populists had no alternative but to go along. Nevertheless, the state Populists nominated a candidate for governor as did the Republicans. For the Democracy, Robert L. Taylor once again came forward to "save" the party from defeat and won the nomination without a contest at the convention. Taylor subsequently angered gold bugs by getting on the silver bandwagon but that was the prescription for victory. He defeated his Republican opponent by a narrow margin and the Populist candidate, a distant third, did not influence the outcome of the race. Demonstrating Tennessee's commitment to free silver, the Democratic presidential nominee carried the state despite the candidacies of both a gold Democrat and a Republican.

The election of 1896 was the last time that the Populist party made a serious effort to challenge the political establishment. Although a party structure remained for several years, the demoralizing events over the previous two years doomed the third party to disintegration. Most of the discontented either quietly drifted back into the Democratic party or succumbed to apathy. The regulars had beaten back the upstart Populists as they had the earlier Alliance and even with Taylor in the governor's chair, the Bourbons remained dominant in the state. Taylor was replaced by a regular, Benton McMillin in 1898. Senator Harris died in 1897 but he was succeeded by another stalwart, Thomas Battle Turley, and Senator Bate was reelected in 1899. Thus the century closed with the Bourbon coalition stronger than ever.

When the Redeemers faltered on state credit, the Bourbons, after a period of quiescence, achieved the ascendancy. The conservative coalition retained power by convincing the electorate that they were the defenders of Southern mores against threats from Republicans, Whiggish New South men, and the twin manifestations of the agrarian revolt, the Alliance and the Populist party. More important, the Bourbon regulars adjusted and adopted the rubric of reform. The regulars became advocates of the New South creed and they ran away with the Populists' demand for free silver. Thus by reconciling change with tradition, the community of conservative interests maintained its dominance. The Bourbons, however, soon faced an ever greater menace, progressivism.

Chapter 3

The Progressives

At the beginning of the twentieth century, the nation entered an age known as the progressive era. The term progressivism is as elusive of definition as Bourbonism and Populism. The earliest interpretation of the movement was simple: after a generation of abuses by big business and machine politics along with the rise of a host of social ills, the nation began to reform its political and economic institutions in the years after the turn of the century. There was an element of truth in that view. The Progressive movement encompassed a variety of concerns: regulation of big business to end the abuses of monopolies; reforming the electoral process to end machine politics to ensure good government; improving working and living conditions to achieve social justice; and extending governmental responsibilities over a wide range of public services. Because of the variety of interests, progressivism cannot be regarded as a social movement in the strict definition of that term. There was no single platform, no established leadership, and no disciplined organization. Progressives could not agree on goals and single interest groups often differed among themselves in degree of emphasis on their priorities. Progressivism was a national mood, a spirit of an age, rather than an organized movement.

Historians cannot agree as to the origins of progressivism. Originally, it was viewed as a direct descendant of Populism, or as William Allen White suggested, progressivism was merely Populism with its whiskers shaved off. It is true that progressives adopted many of the demands of populism such as the progressive income tax, direct election of senators, and the secret ballot as well as the public service concept of government and demands for social justice. Yet a direct relationship between the two movements is hard to find. Perhaps the best that can be said is that the discontent in rural America in the 1890s spawned progressivism. Historians also disagree as to whether the movement was in fact progressive or in reality regressive. There is no agreement on leadership. It has been argued on the one hand that the leaders were men of wealth who were experiencing "status anxiety" and on the other that they came from the upwardly mobile who were experiencing "mobility anxiety." Whatever the case, leaders of progressivism tended to come from the middle class and to be more urban than rural.

Early descriptions and interpretations of progressivism ignored the South, thus intimating that the movement had little or no impact on the region. But Arthur Link's seminal work in the 1940s and C. Vann Woodward's subsequent findings demonstrated conclusively that progressivism was both strong and pervasive in the South. Southern progressivism differed, it seems, in two aspects. Southerners were more concerned with issues of public morals, especially prohibition. More important, Southerners stressed the need to disfranchise blacks in order to purify the electoral process. For a generation, many Southerners argued that Negroes constituted a great mass of ignorant, venal voters who were easily manipulated by corrupt white bosses and this debauched politics. No doubt the fact that blacks tended to vote Republican was the primary concern of Democrats. Whatever the reason, in a number of Southern states, statutory disfranchisement of blacks was regarded as one of the major achievements of the progressive era. But in the process, many poor whites were eliminated from participation in the political institution.

Tennessee did not follow the deep South pattern of disfranchising blacks by statutes. Although some Tennesseans regarded removing Negroes from the political process as essential, the proposal elicited no strong support across the state. There were several reasons for this. First, the black voting population was not large enough to threaten white hegemony in statewide races. Black votes were also useful to white political machines. Besides, black voting was controlled or eliminated by economic pressures or intimidation, the poll tax, and the institution of the white primary. Tennessee's progressives did, however, complete the social separation of the races by legislating segregation in public facilities. In other ways, the Volunteer State reflected the Southern and national progressive norm.

Progressivism permeated the Volunteer State. As elsewhere, reformers were confidently optimistic about their ability to improve, if not perfect the social environment. At the turn of the century, as Joe Michael Shaham has noted, "a new era of progress beckoned to those who would make the necessary commitments and sacrifices" to make the dream of a better world a reality. As it seemed all across the nation, progressivism in Tennessee appeared to rise from the grass roots. Nowhere is this more clearly seen than in Memphis. At the beginning of the twentieth century, the Bluff City was truly Sodom and Gomorrah; crime and vice seemed rampant, filth, disease and poverty widespread, city services far from adequate, and corrupt bosses ruled the community. Memphis was therefore ripe for reform, and William D. Miller traces the movement in that city and demonstrates that the progressive mood was a potent force in the community. A youthful band of civic-minded citizens, with men like Kenneth Douglas McKellar and Edward Hull Crump in the forefront, took the initiative to improve life in Memphis. There were ventures into social reform with mixed results. More important were efforts to improve and expand city services. Commission government was adopted and under the leadership of Mayor Ed Crump, efficient city administration was achieved, city services were vastly improved, but at modest cost to the taxpayers. Memphis was not completely cleaned up—some of the dirt was merely swept into the corner—but it was a different community and life was improved. Other Tennessee cities, Nashville, Chattanooga, and Knoxville have not been scholarly examined but there is evidence that the progressive spirit affected those communities. It may be assumed, however, that reformism had less success in improving conditions in those cities.

Progressivism quickly spread across the state and by 1908, Tennessee was awash with reform movements. It would be no great ex-

aggeration to suggest that virtually everyone gave lip service to some
degree to reform. Even vested interests pressing certain demands
could rationalize their goals with progress. As elsewhere, the drive
for reform was fragmented; there were many individuals and
groups with single goals, often reluctant to coalesce with others.
Various groups were concerned with expanding public services such
as conservation of natural resources, providing good roads, promoting public health programs, and establishing better educational opportunities. The last was one area of reform that virtually
every progressive agreed needed attention, and indeed significant
changes were made in education in Tennessee. There were strong
currents in the state aimed at promoting social justice and public
morality. Goals included curbing vice and crime, prison reform and
establishing a juvenile justice system, ending child labor, and prohibiting the manufacture, sale, and consumption of alcoholic beverages. The last, ironically, sprang from rural Tennessee and
ultimately became, in the words of George Brown Tindall, the "sum
of Progressivism" in the state. Other progressives were outspoken
in calling attention to Tennessee's outmoded constitution that resulted in an inadequate tax structure and promoted waste, inefficiency, and even ineptness in state government. It was difficult,
however, to achieve consensus as to the changes necessary to improve the fundamental law. Still others regarded democracy and
honesty in government as the most important goal to be achieved.
Women's suffrage was an aggressive movement in the Volunteer
State, but quarrels among the leadership and over immediate goals
inhibited the suffragettes. Almost everyone agreed that Tennessee
should institute mandatory party primaries, but the faction in power
at any given time was reluctant to give up control of the party. Finally, the longtime demand to regulate business, banking, and
public utilities, especially railroads, remained strong. But proposed corporate regulation, perhaps more than any area of concern, resulted in intense political conflict. More important, the
progressive mood was not compatible with the conservative inclinations of the dominant political element in Tennessee, the Bourbon regulars.

  Although internal conflict and shifting alliances remained
characteristic of the Democracy, the loose and unstable coalition of

Bourbon regulars continued to be the dominant political element in the state. The governor's office was in safe hands. Benton McMillin, Robert L. Taylor's successor in 1899, was renominated and reelected in 1900 with only token opposition. In 1902, the Democrats nominated for governor James Beriah Frazier, a Chattanooga attorney who had never held an elective office. Frazier's ancestors were planters but his father had been a Unionist and supporter of Andrew Johnson. Nevertheless, the nominee's record of loyalty and service to the party led to his acceptance into the regular camp and Frazier easily defeated his Republican opponent in the general election. Under normal circumstances, Tennesseans rewarded governors with a second term and in 1904, Frazier retained his post with virtually no opposition.

Both United States Senate seats were occupied by Bourbons. When Senator Isham G. Harris died in 1897, Governor Taylor had the responsibility of appointing an interim successor until the legislature could elect someone to fill the unexpired term. An aspirant to that office, the governor must have been sorely tempted to resign with the agreement that his gubernatorial successor appoint him to the post. Political wisdom, however, dictated against that course. If Taylor cannot be identified as a full-fledged Bourbon by this point, the pragmatic governor was cooperating with the regulars. He therefore appointed Thomas B. Turley, a longtime Bourbon loyalist, to the Senate. When the General Assembly met in special session the following year, Turley was elected to the unexpired term despite a concerted effort by Benton McMillin to win the post. Attention then shifted to the seat occupied by William B. Bate, whose term expired in March 1899. Governor Taylor announced as a candidate but when a boom failed to materialize, the old Confederate general was reelected without challenge.

Shortly, attention shifted back to Turley who announced that he would not seek a full term. A number of hopefuls including Governor McMillin lofted trial balloons, but all withdrew when the congressman from Memphis, Edward Ward Carmack, a former journalist and Bourbon, outdistanced the pack. Carmack was nominated by the Democrats in caucus, was easily elected by the legislature, and took his seat in the Senate in March 1901. Even with Bate and Carmack secure for the moment, two popular leaders,

Taylor and McMillin, awaited an opportunity to challenge for the Senate. Indeed, there were rumors that the two aspirants had an informal agreement to avoid conflicting challenges and subsequent events seemed to lend credibility to the rumors. In any event, when Bate came up for reelection in 1905, Taylor remained on the sidelines and McMillin announced against the incumbent. Mc-Millin developed an early commanding lead in commitments by local leaders but Bate's forces eventually beat back the threat and the incumbent won reelection in early 1905. Thus the regulars maintained hegemony beyond the turn of the century but in addition to the turmoil caused by personal ambitions, the philosophically conservative Bourbons were confronted with the reform impetus. Indeed, concessions to progress had to be made. Measures improving education in Tennessee were enacted under Governor McMillin and a mine safety act was passed during Governor Frazier's term. Nevertheless, conflicting personal ambitions and anxiety caused by pressure for reform forced the Bourbon regulars to commit a major blunder in 1905.

In March 1905, Senator Bate died less than five days after he had been sworn in to another term. The Democratic State Executive Committee, controlled by Governor Frazier, called a legislative caucus to nominate a successor. Because the General Assembly was then in session, the caucus met quickly, nominated Frazier, and within two weeks, the legislature had elected the governor to succeed Bate. A regular and an ally, John Isaac Cox, speaker of the State Senate, succeeded Frazier as governor. The haste in electing Frazier to the Senate drew criticism even from the governor's friends. The loudest voice in protest came from Robert L. Taylor, who, if indeed he had an informal agreement with McMillin, was next in line to try for the Senate. Taylor charged that the "snap caucus" had deprived anyone else of the opportunity to mount a candidacy for the Senate. Sensing that he had a good issue to exploit, Taylor announced as a candidate for the Senate seat occupied by Carmack. He charged that the incumbent had participated in the conspiracy to deny others an opportunity to try for the Senate after Bate's death. The point was telling. Carmack, because he was an ally of both Governor Cox and Senator Frazier, had to share the guilt of the "snap caucus" by association.

The senatorial race was long and bitter but it was exciting. Both were gifted speakers who drew large, appreciative crowds. The contest provided a significant innovation. The State Democratic Executive Committee abandoned the caucus for the first time and set a primary in 1906 to determine the senatorial nominee. Taylor garnered the nomination, winning by some 7,000 votes out of approximately 123,000 cast. The victor's margin came as a result of winning the urban vote while Carmack took the rural vote. Even though the customary convention would select the party's nominee for governor, an intense fight for the nomination ran concurrently with the senatorial contest. Governor Cox sought to win a term on his own but he was hurt by the "snap caucus" that had put him in office. The supporters of Malcolm Rice "Ham" Patterson, a Memphis attorney, seized control of the convention and secured the nomination for him. Patterson went on to defeat his Republican opponent in the general election in November 1906, and Taylor was easily elected to the Senate the following January by the General Assembly. Thus the old Bourbon coalition collapsed with the defeats of Cox and Carmack. The regulars had controlled both Senate seats since 1887 and had effectively dominated state government since 1882. Yet, while the election of Patterson to the governorship indicated philosophical departures from the recent past, his assumption of that office reflected a willingness of conservatives to adjust to the times.

Governor Patterson's ancestors were staunchly Bourbon but his father, Josiah Patterson, for some reason, committed heresy to his kind by advocating a hard money policy during the 1890s. By the time of his election as governor, Malcolm Patterson had adjusted to the progressive mood of the times. In both his platform and his actions as governor, he was clearly a progressive reformer. He advocated a variety of measures designed to improve public services and establish social justice and as governor, Patterson achieved some success. The state's educational system was significantly improved, a state pure food and drug law prohibiting the manufacture of adulterated food and false labeling of products was enacted, a new general election law was passed, a state board of elections was created, a highway commission established, and a state reformatory for boys was authorized. Patterson's commitment to reform, however, should not be exaggerated. He was basically conservative and as with so many progressives, he went just far enough to satisfy the public whims of the moment. Patterson revealed a touch of Whiggery in his ideological inclination. On the one hand he pressed for better public services but he was reluctant to push for business regulation. Some of his most important benefactors and supporters were business and railroad managers and Patterson drew back from proposals urging greater regulation of public utilities. Even so, the achievements of his administration might have been even greater had not the temperance movement sidetracked progressivism in Tennessee.

Historian C. Vann Woodward has written that "Partly by chance the prohibition crusade made juncture with the progressive movement in the South." He also noted that it "was primarily a countryman's cause." The observation seems accurate in the case of Tennessee. Efforts to end or eliminate the manufacture, sale, and consumption of intoxicating beverages in the state were of long duration and were indeed rural in origin. The movement to end the liquor traffic gained momentum in the latter half of the nineteenth century. It has been suggested that the temperance crusade originated in rural America as a manifestation of anxiety over the increasing power of urban America. Whatever the source of the movement, it was spawned in the countryside in the Volunteer State and on no other issue was conflict between city and country more clearly delineated. The temperance crusaders won a major victory in 1877 with the enactment of the "Four Mile Law" which prohibited saloons in rural areas within four miles of chartered schools. That measure was amended from time to time so that by 1907, all of rural Tennessee was legally dry; only the urban areas remained wet. Interestingly, prohibition had never been a major issue in a statewide political race. It appeared that the crusaders achieved success only because the political decision makers acquiesced to get rid of an annoying issue. Nevertheless, with organizations such as the Antisaloon League and the Women's Christian Temperance Union taking the lead, the prohibitionists were aggressive, singleminded in purpose, and determined to rid the state, once and for all, of "demon rum." Ironically, the prohibitionists had long advocated local option as "the foot in the door" approach to end the liquor traffic. By 1908, however, the drys, anticipating success, now abandoned local option for mandatory statewide prohibition. The wets, on the other hand, long opponents of local option, switched and now took that position as a means to prevent prohibition in the cities. What the temperance crusaders needed to achieve success was dynamic leadership. They found their leader in Edward Ward Carmack.

A brilliant journalist, Carmack early won fame as editor of two Nashville newspapers before going on to Memphis in the early 1890's to edit first the *Commercial* and then the *Commercial Appeal*. In 1896, he was elected to Congress as an advocate of free silver, defeating the "gold bug" Josiah Patterson, father of Governor Malcolm Patterson. Four years later he was promoted to the Senate where he won national recognition as an eloquent opponent of imperialism. Charismatic, Carmack developed an intensely loyal following in Tennessee. His defeat by Robert L. Taylor in 1906 was therefore a bitter experience for Carmack and his loyalists. In hopes of an early restoration to a position of responsibility, his followers began pressing Carmack to challenge Patterson for the governorship in 1908. No doubt Bourbon conservatives, fearful that Patterson would put together an unbeatable coalition, urged Carmack to run to prevent that eventuality. Prohibitionists also prevailed upon Carmack to take the lead in their cause and run on a temperance platform. Normally, Tennesseans rewarded governors who had avoided disruptive issues with a second term. Because Patterson had been successful in his first term and nothing had marred the political serenity in the state, he would thus be hard to beat. Nevertheless, Carmack, bitter over his defeat by Taylor, anxious for vindication, and perhaps deceived by the enthusiasm of his loyalists for a race against Patterson, committed himself to a campaign against the incumbent governor. The Democratic State Executive Committee, in anticipation of a good race, set a delegated primary rather than a convention to determine the nominee.

The Democratic gubernatorial race of 1908 proved to be a bitter and divisive one. Because of Patterson's successful record and progressive stance, Carmack was forced to offer a similar platform. Lacking a significant issue, the challenger accepted the importuning of the temperance forces and came out in favor of mandatory

statewide prohibition. Patterson, having the support of the wets and
the liquor industry, advocated local option. The most exciting feature of the campaign was a series of some fifty debates between the
candidates. Because Carmack pressed the issue, prohibition was the
most discussed point in the debates. But Carmack was not known
as a teetotaler and Patterson was able to demonstrate that the challenger was merely an opportunist on the issue. When the primary
votes were counted, Patterson won in a close race by about 7,000
votes. The incumbent carried the urban areas; the challenger's votes
were mostly from rural areas. The campaign left the Democratic
party bitterly divided but Patterson earned another term in the
general election, in part because Republicans were just as divided.

Although prohibition was the most discussed issue in the Democratic gubernatorial primary, the outcome was by no means a referendum on the liquor question. Other factors were important, not
the least of which was the incumbent's image as a progressive; his
program was more acceptable to the increasing number of reform-
minded groups. Even so, the opponents of "demon rum" refused
to accept defeat and became even more aggressive and shrill in their
crusade to achieve complete prohibition. The unquestioned leader
of the temperance forces was Carmack, and in September 1908 he
returned to journalism as editor of the *Nashville Tennessean*. The
newspaper was published by the flamboyant Luke Lea, a rising
power in the Democratic party in the midstate area. The publisher
had supported Taylor for the Senate and Patterson for governor
in 1906 but soon broke with the latter. He joined the temperance
crusade and endorsed Carmack for governor in 1908.

Soon after assuming his post on the *Tennessean*, Carmack
launched a vituperative and vicious editorial campaign against the
incumbent governor. Rather than emphasizing Patterson's alliance
with the liquor industry, the editor charged that the governor had
established a corrupt political machine. Shortly, for some reason,
Carmack singled out for special abuse Colonel Duncan Cooper, one
of Governor Patterson's close advisors. Cooper had given Carmack
his first significant position in journalism in 1886 and the two remained friends and political allies for years. But when Cooper supported Taylor in the Senate race in 1906, the longtime friendship
was broken. The bitter Carmack began referring to Cooper in his

editorials as the little "bald headed angel of Hell" and as "major," implying that Cooper's promotion to colonel in the Confederate army was fraudulent. Then on November 8, the editor penned an especially brutal castigation of his former friend. An angry Cooper sent Carmack a threat and both men armed themselves. The controversy had reached the flash point. The aggressive Carmack, rather than halting the rhetorical attacks to prevent tragedy, persisted and the following day another vicious editorial appeared. Cooper had had enough. That afternoon, Cooper, accompanied by his son, Robin, confronted Carmack on a street in downtown Nashville. Although the editor drew first and fired two shots that grazed Robin, the latter was more accurate and Carmack was killed instantly. Carmack's total commitment to the anti-liquor crusade may be questioned but the prohibitionists now had a martyr.

It has been suggested that Carmack was more influential in death than in life. The assessment seems accurate. The manner of his death stunned Tennessee and the nation. The temperance groups, led by a screaming, shrill press, charged that the killing of the editor was the result of a conspiracy by the advocates of "demon rum" and mobilized public opinion for prohibition. Intense pressure was brought to bear on the General Assembly which convened in January 1909, and mandatory statewide prohibition was enacted over Governor Patterson's veto. In addition, the legislature weakened the governor's control over election machinery in the state. Simultaneously with the enactment of prohibition, the Coopers were charged with murder and brought to trial in an inflamed atmosphere. The jury in the trial, which was both a comic opera and a kangaroo court, convicted and sentenced both Duncan and Robin Cooper to lengthy prison terms.

Nearly a year later, the State Supreme Court, after reviewing the case, overturned Robin's conviction on a technicality but upheld the conviction of his father. Almost immediately, in an act that he must have known was tantamount to political suicide, Governor Patterson pardoned Duncan Cooper. The prohibition groups were furious as expected, but some of the governor's loyalists were upset with his precipitous action and the liquor industry now regarded him as a liability. Even so, Patterson controlled the Democratic party's machinery. When the State Executive Committee set a guber-

natorial primary in 1910, Patterson, hoping to become the first
governor since the Civil War to serve three terms, announced as a
candidate. But anti-administration and temperance forces boycotted the primary and the governor was renominated by default.
Meanwhile, the anti-liquor element won control of the Republican
party and nominated Ben Wade Hooper of Newport in East Tennessee. Prohibition Democrats, led by Luke Lea and Edward Bushrod Stahlmen, publisher of the *Nashville Banner*, endorsed Hooper.
Facing inevitable defeat, Patterson withdrew and the Executive
Committee persuaded a reluctant Senator Taylor to run once again
and try to "save" the party from defeat. Time had, no doubt, taken
a toll, but Taylor traveled widely, again attracting audiences with
florid oratory and charm. He endorsed some of the important progressive priorities such as good roads, good government, and better schools. But the rift in the Democracy was too deep this time
and the old conciliator was unable to prevent defeat. To prohibition Democrats, Taylor was merely a tool of the Patterson administration. The unlikely fusion alliance held firm and Hooper won
the governor's office with fifty-two percent of the votes out of almost 255,000 cast. Thus for only the second time since Reconstruction, a Republican had won the governor's office in Tennessee.

The temperance crusaders had won. The manufacture, transportation, and sale of intoxicating beverages had been banned in
the Volunteer State. Moreover, an alliance of prohibitionist Democrats and Republicans was in political control of the state. But
Tennessee was in turmoil. The viciousness of Carmack's campaign
against the liquor industry and the Patterson administration, the
nature of his death, and the pardoning of Duncan Cooper divided
families, friends, and communities and the Democratic party was
in disarray. It was no momentary condition; a residue of bitterness
remained for many years. Conflict erupted early in Hooper's
administration when thirty-four prohibitionist legislators fled the
state to break a quorum and prevent passage of an election law that
would have given control of election machinery in the state to the
regular Democratic organization. A compromise was eventually
worked out but harmony was not achieved.

Although there were disputes among the fusionists, the alliance
remained strong enough to elect publisher Luke Lea to the United

States Senate to replace James B. Frazier, the product of the "snap caucus" and the last of the old Democratic "regulars." Anti-prohibitionist Democrats were still active and nominated former chief executive Benton McMillin for the governorship in 1912. He campaigned for modification of the liquor laws. Faced with the possibility of repeal, prohibitionist Democrats once again joined with Republicans to reelect Hooper, but his margin of victory was only 8,000 out of 241,000 votes cast. Ironically, in the exciting three-way presidential race that year, Democrats coalesced behind Thomas Woodrow Wilson, the Democratic nominee. Wilson carried the state with a majority of the votes over Progressive Republican Theodore Roosevelt and the incumbent President William Howard Taft. The unity in support of the Democratic presidential nominee did not indicate restoration of harmony. The rift in the party was far from being healed. Thus at the time when the progressive movement was, perhaps, at the high water mark, the dominant party in Tennessee was badly split.

An authority on Tennessee in the progressive era, Joe Michael Shahan, suggests that Governor Hooper was a farsighted progressive and the state's "most effective reform leader." Perhaps he was. He spoke the rhetoric of reform and tried to mold the fusionists into an effective reform instrument. Hooper pressed a number of progressive priorities and during his administration, some of the achievements of Patterson's tenure were modestly expanded. His greatest claim as a progressive was his efforts for prohibition and more effective law enforcement. Aside from the problem of dealing with the partisan Democratic majority in the legislature, albeit a fractious one, Hooper's preoccupation with temperance reform weakened efforts to achieve other reforms. The governor was not alone; he had plenty of allies helping to make prohibition "the sum of progressivism" in Tennessee.

Prohibition remained an issue largely because it proved almost impossible to obtain compliance. Moonshine continued to be made and saloons in the cities remained in operation because political leaders such as Mayor Ed Crump of Memphis refused to enforce state law. Frustrated temperance leaders began to urge more effective enforcement measures. Governor Hooper took the initiative when the General Assembly convened in 1913 by offering a series of measures for enforcement. One act stipulated that saloons could be declared public nuisances and forced to close and others authorized removal from office local political leaders who failed to enforce state law. In a bitter struggle, anti-prohibition forces blocked passage of the measures. Conflict erupted again over attempts by Democrats to amend the election laws.

Undaunted, Hooper tried again to implement enforcement of prohibition by calling the legislature into special session in September 1913. The session was a bitter battleground between the temperance side and the opponents of prohibition. At one point, both sides brought armed men into the legislative chambers and a riot occurred on the floor of the House on another occasion. Although a majority of the General Assembly appeared to be favorable to the enforcement measures, opponents succeeded in preventing them from coming to a vote and the session ended without passage. Governor Hooper immediately called another extraordinary session. Temperance forces mounted a massive lobbying campaign and the opposition finally conceded defeat and the governor's enforcement measures became law. The joy of the prohibitionists was unrestrained. Unfortunately, despite vigorous efforts on the part of administration officials assisted by private groups, saloons in the cities remained open and continued to dispense liquor. Still, the Democrats were coming to the point of accepting the will of the electorate.

Efforts to reestablish unity in the Democracy began soon after the enactment of the prohibition enforcement measures. The harmony movement met resistance because much bitterness remained. But enough anti-prohibition Democrats acquiesced in the popular will and a reunited party nominated Thomas Clark Rye, the relatively unknown attorney general of the thirteenth district and a prohibitionist, for governor in 1914. Temperance Democrats, believing that Rye's commitment to the anti-liquor crusade was genuine, defected the fusionist organization and returned to the fold. Despite a concerted effort by the Republicans and remnant fusionists to reelect Hooper to a third term, Rye won the governorship by 21,000 votes out of more than 254,000 cast, a clear majority. Democrats also won control of the General Assembly.

In the legislative session in 1915, Governor Rye endorsed a measure to strengthen enforcement of prohibition. Known as the Ouster Law, the proposal provided means whereby local officials could be removed for failure to enforce the anti-liquor laws. Indicative of the commitment of the reunited Democratic party to prohibition, the measure passed the General Assembly by an overwhelming majority. The measure was soon used. First, Mayor Hilary Howse of Nashville and then Mayor Ed Crump of Memphis were ousted from office for failing to try to eliminate the liquor traffic in their cities. The latter long blamed the utility magnates for his removal from office because he had championed public ownership of power, gas, and street railway services. Perhaps, but removal was part of the prohibition agenda. Other public officials in the state were removed under the ouster law or were impeached for failure to enforce the liquor laws. With conditions back to normal and, in the tradition of Tennessee politics, Rye won renomination and reelection in 1916 overwhelmingly.

Having the initiative and heady with success, the temperance forces secured the enactment of even more stringent anti-liquor laws in 1917 and the city saloons finally began to close. The end of "demon rum" seemed assured when the Eighteenth Amendment to the United States Constitution was ratified in 1920. With the liquor question settled and despite the distractions of World War I, Rye's administration and the legislature addressed one of the priorities of the progressives: election reform. In 1917, the General Assembly mandated primary nominations for statewide offices. In addition, the registration of automotive vehicles was required and a tax to match federal highway funds was established.

Having made peace with the temperance issue, the Democracy began to reassert its dominance in Tennessee. In 1915, Congressman Kenneth McKellar of Memphis won the Democratic senatorial nomination in a bitter contest with incumbent Luke Lea. McKellar went on to become the state's first popularly elected senator, easily defeating former governor, Ben Hooper, in the general election in 1916. Two years later John Knight Shields, who had been elected to the Senate by the General Assembly in 1913, narrowly defeated Governor Rye in the primary but won the general election over Republican H. Clay Evans by a substantial margin. In the

Democratic gubernatorial race in 1918, Chancellor Albert Houston Roberts of Overton County won the nomination by a slender margin over Austin Peay of Clarksville. Roberts had no difficulty in winning the general election.

With the prohibition question apparently settled, Democrats began to focus attention on some of the long-ignored items on the progressive agenda. In 1920, for example, a special session of the General Assembly ratified the proposed Nineteenth or woman suffrage amendment. As the thirty-sixth state to ratify the amendment, Tennessee thus earned the distinction of insuring that it became a part of the Constitution of the United States. More important was Governor Roberts's bold attempt at tax reform. Tennessee's antiquated tax structure, long a principal concern of many progressives, was inefficient, plagued by incompetent and corrupt collectors, and produced inadequate revenue to meet the state's growing need for services. The governor's tax package provided for a "sliding scale" assessment and expansion of the power of the Railroad Commission and giving that agency authority to assess taxes on public utilities such as water, gas, power, and telegraph and telephone companies. Roberts believed that the new system would reduce levies on those less able to pay and tap sources of revenue that had previously evaded taxation. After a struggle, the legislature enacted the reform package. The new system was, however, unpopular and it soon became apparent that it would not produce the desired effect; evasions continued and it appeared that property taxes would inevitably increase. The Democratic party was by no means a homogeneous entity. The party still contained a variety of elements and as always, its dominance in Tennessee was uneasy at best. Roberts's tax program became a volatile issue that threatened to split the Democracy, and the governor himself seemed vulnerable as the election of 1920 approached.

Despite Roberts's unpopularity, none of the available possibilities were willing to become involved in the controversy over taxation. The governor's only opposition for the Democratic nomination was a little-known former mayor of Chattanooga. In a low voter turnout, the incumbent won renomination but his margin of victory was anything but comfortable. The conflict within the Democratic party gave hope to the Republicans and the chance to win the governor's office improved when the popular old war-horse and veteran of the "war of the roses," Alf Taylor, garnered the nomination. Taylor campaigned vigorously. In his public appearances, he played the fiddle, accompanied by a quartet of singers, and he entertained audiences with stories about his hunting dog, "Old Limber." He did not, however, completely ignore issues. The voters were frequently reminded that Roberts was the architect of the hated tax program. Roberts was further handicapped when several prominent Democrats withheld endorsement and sat out the race. When the votes were counted, Taylor had won the governorship by a large majority.

A number of factors contributed to the Republican victory in 1920. It was a banner year for Republicans across the nation. Taking advantage of widespread dissatisfaction with the national and international policies of Wilson's Democratic administration, the Grand Old Party won control of Congress and elected a president. No doubt some of the dissatisfaction spilled over into Tennessee state politics. There was also a residue of unhappiness over the ratification of the woman suffrage amendment. The most important factor in the Republican victory in the Volunteer State was taxation, which had caused a rift in the Democracy. Finally, in the popular Taylor, the Republicans had the right candidate at the right time. He was not, however, an effective governor because of division within his own party and the hostility of the Democratic legislature. The outcome of the governor's race once again demonstrated that the Republicans could win statewide races only when Democrats were not united. Thus, as the Progressive Era closed, the dominant Democracy remained a party of amorphous, ever-shifting factions and coalitions, prone to internecine conflict.

After the turn of the century, Tennesseans boarded the progressive bandwagon. Various groups recognized the existence of numerous social problems and there seemed to be no end to proposed solutions. Such was the mood that almost everyone was, in regard to a special interest at least, a progressive. The political system had, by 1907, begun to address many of the items on the progressive agenda. But after 1908, prohibition became the most important progressive goal. The minority temperance groups viewed drinking as the greatest social evil. A ban on the manufac-

ture and use of intoxicating beverages would, in turn, they believed, correct a host of social and political evils. The temperance
crusade may well have become a major concern eventually but its
juncture with progressivism in Tennessee was almost an aberration. Led by Carmack, the politicians seized prohibition less for
moral reasons than as an issue to use in an attempt to secure political power. Carmack's vindictive attack on Duncan Cooper had
nothing directly to do with the liquor question. The nature of his
death mobilized the temperance crusaders to a greater effort and
prohibition became law. Enforcement, however, remained a problem. For almost a decade, the political system in Tennessee focused
attention on the almost consuming issue of "demon rum." Thus
prohibition distracted Tennesseans and diverted their energies
from other progressive goals. Government reform, tax reform, and
a host of social needs were, in large measure, ignored. Ironically,
all the efforts to end the liquor traffic and purify society went for
nought. As the saloons in the cities closed, illicit traffic increased in
proportion and in the 1920s, Tennessee became a major producer
of "moonshine" whiskey. Then in 1933, the prohibition amendment to the national constitution was repealed and before the decade ended, the Tennessee legislature legalized beer and permitted
local option on the sale of whisky. Within a generation, Tennessee
had revoked prohibition and returned to conditions that existed in
1908.

    In politics, much changed between 1900 and 1920, but much
remained the same. Although continuously challenged, the old
regulars dominated the power structure in Tennessee's Democratic party as the new century dawned. This Bourbon hegemony
self-destructed in the "snap caucus" scandal. Even if it had not, the
demand for reform would have, sooner or later, overwhelmed the
conservative ascendancy. The introduction of the issue of prohibition complicated matters. The decade after 1908 was one of confusion as the lines delineating ideological persuasion blurred.
Eventually the conservative establishment adjusted and accepted
reform. As George Brown Tindall has suggested, "the ultimate
achievement of the Bourbons was that of all durable conservative
movements: the reconciliation of tradition with innovation." By
1920, the Bourbons had become urban progressives. Despite the
Republican victory that year, a new era of dominance by the Bour-
bon-urban-progressives was on the horizon.

Chapter 4

City
vs.
Country

The progressive era was a transitional period in Tennessee. The economic and demographic landscape in the state was significantly altered between 1900 and 1920. From its inception, the Volunteer State was a predominantly agricultural state but the process of industrialization began after the Civil War. The pace was slow but as early as 1890 the wealth produced by manufacturing exceeded that of farming. The rate of industrial growth accelerated after the turn of the century and the advent of World War I further stimulated the increase in manufacturing establishments. Because of mineral resources, timber, and water power sites, East Tennessee's industrial growth was significantly greater than the rest of the state. For Tennessee as a whole, by 1920, the value of manufactured goods was more than double that of farm products. The trend in industrial development continued in the decade of the 1920s.

In spite of the rise in manufacturing, farming remained, long after 1920, the single most important economic activity in the state. Yet farming, especially for the small operator, was not a paying proposition. The generation after the Civil War was not a prosperous time for those in agricultural pursuits. The progressive era saw some improvement, especially with the coming of World War I, but after 1920, agriculture slipped back into depression. Tenant farming remained widespread in the middle and western sections of the state and poverty in rural areas was commonplace. The discouraging prospects in agriculture and the lure of jobs in manufacturing contributed to a decline in the number of farmers. By 1920, more than fifty percent of the labor force in Tennessee was still engaged in farming, but the number in industry was growing rapidly. Urban growth, along with a decline in the rural and small town population, was concurrent with the rise of industry. The population increase in cities in East Tennessee was especially great. Knoxville, for example, increased by twenty-four percent between 1900 and 1920. After 1920, cities in Middle and West Tennessee began to experience rapid growth. Thus by 1930, Tennessee was still largely rural and agrarian, but was clearly making the transition to a predominantly urban and industrial state.

The transition was a painful one and brought the city and countryside into conflict. Industrialization and urbanization threatened the status of the time-honored yeoman farmer. The increasing population of the cities and the influence of business and industrial interests eroded the political power of rural and small-town Tennessee. The decline of the farmer began after the Civil War. Agrarian interests were confronted with declining market prices for farm products while interest rates, freight rates, and taxes remained high. Thus the farmer had real grievances but, perhaps, some were imagined. In any case, tillers of the soil therefore sought scapegoats. The managers of industry and their sycophants in government were blamed for the plight of the farmer. Cities, because they were centers of industry and other forces that suppressed farmers, shared the blame. Moreover, cities that were governed by cynical, corrupt political bosses, were havens for the sins of liquor, prostitution, and gambling, and blasphemous ideas that were foreign to rural values. Agrarians in the late nineteenth century rose in protest but the revolt was beaten back by the entrenched political establishment rather than the cities. The grievances of farmers were not resolved. The prohibition movement was a manifestation of rural discontent and anxiety with the rapid economic and social changes taking place.

The social and economic changes of the progressive era and the rising tide of urbanization were factors in the revival of the Ku Klux Klan and the almost frantic crusade of the religious fundamentalists against "modernism" in the 1920s. This is illustrated in the attack on the theory of evolution and the subsequent "monkey trial" of John Thomas Scopes in Dayton, Tennessee, in 1925. Yet in spite of paranoiac fears, the countryside held the political trumps in the Volunteer State. The constitution of 1870 required legislative reapportionment every ten years, but only once, in 1901, was representation reapportioned. The rural block beat back all attempts to apportion according to population. The result was that cities became increasingly underrepresented in the General Assembly. For more than a generation after 1920, the countryside controlled the law-making body in Tennessee and all attempts to change representation, or for that matter the revenue system and appropriations that favored rural areas, met with failure. Moreover, the governors were rural in outlook. Cities could elect a state chief executive only if the countryside was divided. Many of the political battles in the half century after 1920 involved conflict between the cities and the country as the latter sought to protect its advantages. Issues not involving the rural-urban conflict reflected the nature of the political structure in Tennessee. The dominant Democratic party was a collection of factions and shifting alliances of local or regional organizations. Like the Democrats, the Republicans were not homogeneous. The minority party contained numerous factions but was essentially divided into two groups, the racially mixed Black and Tans and the white supremacists, the Lily Whites. The former, led by second district Congressman James Willis Taylor, was the stronger of the two for many years after 1920. Taylor was, in effect, a state boss, controlling Republican patronage. One of his important allies was Robert R. Church, Jr., boss of the black community in Memphis. Church had a voice in federal patronage in the city and was a power in the Republican party at both the state and national levels. The unwillingness of Taylor, Church, and other Black and Tans to share power was the main reason why, for half a century after 1920, the Grand Old Party was weak and unable to effectively challenge the Democrats.

Tennessee's Democratic party contained a plethora of local or county machines, or as one scholar termed them, rural feudal baronies. Often, a number of these baronies were welded together to form a regional organization. City machines had long existed in the state as well, but reflecting the urbanization during the progressive era, the power and influence at the state level of these city organizations rose correspondingly. Ultimately, the most powerful urban machine in Tennessee, and indeed in the nation, was the one put together by Ed Crump in Memphis.

Born in Holly Springs, Mississippi, of Bourbon ancestry, Crump moved to Memphis in the 1890s as a young man and achieved success in business. He entered politics in the early part of the century as a progressive reformer. Elected mayor in 1909, he gave the Bluff City an efficient administration and expanded services at low cost to the taxpayers. His ouster in 1915 for failing to enforce prohibition had little effect on his popularity in Memphis, and over the following decade the charismatic Crump fused together the city's ethnic groups, including the black community, and white middle- and upper-class businessmen into a powerful machine. As the 1920s progressed, his influence was increasingly felt at the state level. The Memphis boss was allied with Senator McKellar. A native of Alabama, and like Crump, from a Bourbon background, McKellar migrated to Memphis in the 1890s. He was an active reformer and after a stint in the House of Representatives, was elected to the Senate in 1916. He put together a loose statewide organization based on patronage and was unbeatable at the polls.

In Nashville, another strong organization was led by the triumvirate of Hilary Howse, Kit T. McConnico, and Edward Bushrod Stahlman. Howse served several terms as mayor and exercised a great deal of power. McConnico directed the machine's organization. Of the three, Stahlman had more influence chiefly because he was the publisher of the *Nashville Banner*. A German immigrant, Stahlman achieved wealth in railroads before purchasing the *Banner* in 1885. The newspaper soon became the organ of the conservative business community in Nashville and the publisher earned a reputation as a hard-hitting, outspoken journalist. The machine, however, did not achieve anywhere near the power of the one in Memphis, perhaps because of the lack of centralized leadership.

More important, there was stiff competition from another organization headed by the flamboyant Luke Lea.

Born in 1879, the scion of a prominent Middle Tennessee family, Lea became active in politics at an early age. He supported Patterson for governor in 1906 but soon broke with him and founded
the *Nashville Tennessean* to oppose the administration. A year later,
he employed Carmack as editor to carry on the fight against Patterson but resumed personal control of the newspaper after the editor's violent death. A leader in the fusionist movement, Lea was
elected to the Senate in 1911 but failed to win renomination in a
contest with McKellar in 1916. During World War I, he was made
a colonel and helped organize an artillery regiment from Tennessee and gained some notoriety shortly after the war for a scheme to
kidnap the German Kaiser from his exile in the Netherlands. Upon
his return to Tennessee, Lea helped organize the American Legion
and soon welded the veterans into a powerful political pressure
group. Thus Lea, with control of a popular newspaper that was
widely circulated in the midstate area, was one of the power brokers in the Volunteer State. In 1922, he helped elect Austin Peay
governor of Tennessee.

The contest for the Democratic gubernatorial nomination involved two principal candidates: the aging former governor Benton McMillin and Austin Peay, a Clarksville attorney. The former
had the support of the Howse-McConnico-Stahlman faction while
the latter was endorsed by Lea. Illness forced Crump to sit out the
campaign. Peay won by 38,000 votes. He polled well in some rural
areas but his margin of victory was the urban vote. Senator Mc-
Kellar had little trouble in his bid for renomination. The incumbent governor, Alf Taylor, had no opposition in the Republican
primary and thus received the nomination. The unfortunate, if not
inept governor tried entertainment on the hustings once again but
it did little good this time. Peay won the governorship by a sizable
majority, demonstrating that the Republican victory in 1920 was
indeed an aberration. At the same time, McKellar had no difficulty
in winning reelection.

Born and raised in Kentucky, Peay began law practice in
Clarksville and served in the legislature. He was Patterson's campaign manager in the governor's race in 1908, but the death of

Carmack and the pardoning of Duncan Cooper disturbed Peay and he retired from politics for a decade. After amassing some wealth, he returned to the political arena in 1918 when he made an unsuccessful bid for the Democratic gubernatorial nomination. If the mood in Tennessee in the 1920s may be characterized as a reaction to the activist, reform impulse of the progressive era, Peay was very much in tune with the times. Conservative by nature, he was not unlike the earlier Bourbons. Reform was not entirely dead and Peay, like many conservatives, became a business progressive.

Achieving both economy and efficiency in government had long been one of the progressive goals. Tennessee was a classic example of waste and inefficiency in government. Compounding the problem was an inequitable tax structure. By the early 1920s, the state was in a near crisis with the state debt rising, revenue declining, and services that were far from adequate. The chaos of Governor Taylor's administration and his inability to improve conditions was the last straw. Realizing that the confusion in state government in Tennessee was not conducive to economic growth, business leaders and their associations and farmer groups took the initiative in demanding reform. Peay's own business experience no doubt made it easier for him to adopt a business progressive platform. At any rate, he accepted the mandate and the General Assembly elected with him in 1922 was agreeable to change.

The underlying problem was the state's outdated constitution. Amending the fundamental law seemed out of the question for the process was time-consuming and cumbersome. Reforming the state's bureaucratic jungle of offices, bureaus, and departments was simpler and easier. Some sixty-four agencies had been created by and were responsible to the General Assembly rather than to the administrative branch of government. Positions in those agencies were patronage plums for legislators. The governor was, in effect, a mere figurehead, rather than an administrator. Moreover, the responsibilities of the various offices often overlapped. The net result was waste and inefficiency. Therefore, after a study by an outside consultant, Governor Peay presented to the General Assembly in 1923 a measure known as the Administration Reorganization Bill. Despite some strong opposition, the measure passed. Under the act, the agencies of state government were combined into eight departments responsible to the governor rather than the legislature. The result was greater efficiency and economy. The measure was revolutionary in that an enormous amount of power in patronage shifted from the General Assembly to the governor's office. Peay's revenue proposal which called for a profits tax on corporations and easing the burden on farmers also passed and revenue receipts increased. The governor then turned his attention to public services. First on the agenda was roads. Despite pressure from contractors and distributors of road-building materials for a bond issue to expedite construction, Peay insisted on the slower pay-as-you-go process supported by a users tax on gasoline. The subsequent increased road construction pleased the countryside.

Governor Peay's first term was a success. In a commanding position and the two-term tradition in his favor, he won renomination and reelection in 1924 handily. In the Senate race that year, General Lawrence Tyson, a hero of World War I, defeated incumbent John K. Shields in the Democratic primary and was elected to the Senate in the general election. In his second term, Peay turned to overhauling the state's educational system. A major reform, enacted in 1925, raised overall educational standards, increased funds for teacher salaries and school construction, and established an equalization fund that was, in effect, a state subsidy for poor counties. The school package was funded by a delegated tax on tobacco. Since most of the tax would be collected in the larger communities, cities were supporting schools in the countryside. Moreover, Peay's educational reforms made Tennessee's schools a state responsibility and centralized control in the hands of the commissioner of education, an appointee of the governor.

Governor Peay had initially been elected by urbanites, and the cities had applauded his efforts at efficiency and economy in government. But his roads program, education package, and other initiatives revealed a rural bias and gradually eroded urban support. Conversely, his support in the countryside increased. With his recently acquired patronage power, Peay put together a coalition of rural baronies and, apparently, he successfully courted support among East Tennessee Republicans. He also maintained his alliance with Luke Lea, but the governor was clearly the dominant partner. Peay had made the governorship a powerful office. The governmental reorganization shifted power from the legislative to the executive branch and educational reforms shifted power from local governments to the state government. As David Lee has noted, he became the first truly effective governor since the Civil War.

Having solidified his power, Peay, in 1926, sought to become the first governor since the Civil War to serve three terms. Because there was some sentiment in the state against third terms, some of the governor's important backers deserted him. He also had a formidable opponent for the Democratic nomination in State Treasurer Hill McAlister of Nashville, who was backed by the Howse-McConnico-Stahlman faction of Nashville and Ed Crump of Memphis. Because of these endorsements, McAlister was known as the candidate of the cities. Peay, playing on the anti-urban bias of his rural constituents, emphasized his opponent's city connections while calling attention to the benefits the countryside reaped from his programs. The race was close and the incumbent won by only 8,000 votes. The primary was significant because the differences between city and county were clearly delineated for the first time. Rural and small-town Tennessee had elected a governor. Urban voters could elect the state's chief executive only when the rural vote was split.

Peay was easily returned to the governorship in the general election but he ran into trouble when the General Assembly met in 1927. For one thing, he was in poor health and the legislature was increasingly restive under his control. It was the delegations from the urban counties, however, that thwarted further implementation of Peay's programs. Then in October 1927, the governor died suddenly. That made Henry Hollis Horton from Marshall County and speaker of the State Senate the state's chief executive. A first-term senator with little political experience, Horton was inept, pliable, and under the influence of Luke Lea. His elevation to the governorship thus made Lea the single most important power broker in Tennessee politics.

Luke Lea had reached the crest of his political power. He had an alliance of local machines, particularly in the middle section of the state and he controlled the *Nashville Tennessean*, a newspaper that was especially influential in that area. He now had a governor he could control. Lea was also allied with Rogers Caldwell, the head of the South's largest financial institution, Caldwell and Company. Although primarily in banking, Caldwell and Company had extensive interests and investments. Lea and Caldwell were jointly involved in a number of banking ventures and the financier backed Lea's acquisition of the Memphis *Commercial Appeal* and the Knoxville *Journal,* purchases that expanded the publisher's influence to other parts of the state. Caldwell's connection with state government through Lea became profitable. For example, a subsidiary of Caldwell and Company was awarded contracts without bids for road building materials. Moreover, state funds were deposited in Caldwell and Company banks. The Lea/Caldwell/Horton combine became a powerful statewide machine. Nevertheless, the opposition gave the machine a scare in the Democratic gubernatorial contest in 1928.

As expected, Horton entered the primary to succeed himself and he had the endorsement of Lea and his newspapers. McAlister entered the race and, as in 1926, had the support of Crump and Stahlman. A third candidate in the primary was Lewis Pope, commissioner of institutions under Governor Peay. Pope had no organizational support but he posed a threat to Horton. The campaign was a bitter contest but Horton survived, defeating McAlister by only 5,000 votes. Once again, McAlister's tallies were largely urban while Horton's were rural. Pope's votes were also from the countryside but were not enough to prevent the incumbent from winning. The primary demonstrated that the rural-urban cleavage remained pronounced. Senator McKellar won renomination easily and both he and Horton had no trouble in the general election.

Events during the legislative session in 1929 provided little comfort for the machine. Led by Crump's Memphis delegation, the forces that had plagued Peay in 1927 harassed Governor Horton. Indeed, virtually all of his program was defeated in the legislative session. By this time, Lea and Crump were bitter enemies but the former had certain advantages. Through Horton, Lea controlled state patronage in Shelby County and could name elections commissioners in Memphis as well as appoint a criminal court judge in the Bluff City hostile to Crump. Without a voice in these appointments, the Memphis boss would indeed have difficulty in main-

taining hegemony in his own county. After the legislative session
in 1929, Lea began pressing Crump to strike a bargain. Crump
agreed to support Horton's legislative program and the governor's
reelection in 1930. In return, he was granted the right to name
election commissioners and the criminal judge in Memphis. When
Governor Horton called the legislature into special session, true to
his word, the Memphis delegation voted with the majority to enact
Horton's tax package and the authorization to sell $10,000,000 in
bonds to expedite highway construction.

Lea emerged the victor. Because Peay's governmental reorganization had provided the administration with increased patronage,
Lea handed out jobs for political purposes in the manner of the most
ruthless of bosses. Such was his control that Horton had only token
opposition in the Democratic primary in 1930 and won by a large
majority. Crump's Memphis gave the governor an overwhelming
vote. There was a unique senatorial contest in 1930, two races for
the same post. Senator Tyson died in 1929 and one race was for the
remaining months of that term. The more important contest was
for the full term. Lea was unable to find an available candidate for
the full term and his implacable foe, Congressman Cordell Hull,
won the nomination easily. Both Horton and Hull were easy victors
in the general election. Despite the governor's reelection, the Lea/
Caldwell/Horton regime was about to crumble.

The Great Depression had begun and many financial institutions around the country were tottering. There were rumors that
Caldwell and Company was having difficulties long before the general election in November 1930. A few days after Horton's reelection, the financial giant collapsed, the result of years of
mismanagement and lax standards. Lea lost his newspapers but the
biggest loser was state government. Tennessee lost over six and a
half million dollars on deposit in Caldwell's banks. Because the empire crossed state lines, a number of state and federal indictments
were handed down against Lea and Caldwell for conspiracy to vi-
olate banking statutes. There was only one conviction: Lea served
a term in a federal prison. In Tennessee, many people quickly came
to the conclusion that Lea, Caldwell, and Horton were thoroughly
dishonest. Calls for an investigation came from all across the state.
The General Assembly which met in January 1931 conducted an

examination of Governor Horton's handling of the state's financial affairs and concluded that there had been numerous instances of mismanagement, waste, and even fraud committed by the administration. The report led to cries for the impeachment of Horton and the leader of the chorus was Ed Crump. The impeachers had an early initiative and appeared to have the votes in the House for conviction. But Horton's supporters convinced many rural Tennesseans that the attack on the administration, led by a corrupt urban boss, was an attempt by the cities to weaken the political power of the countryside. Moreover, Lea mobilized the army of state job holders and contractors who had profited under Horton as lobbyists and impeachment was defeated. Even so, the scandal destroyed the governor and brought about the downfall of Luke Lea. The leader of the state's largest and most efficient political machines, Ed Crump of Memphis, moved to fill the vacuum as the leading power broker in Tennessee.

To many Tennesseans, especially in rural areas, Crump's organization was the symbol of all that was evil in the cities. The machine shielded vice and crime, took payoffs, and practiced fraud in elections by trucking large numbers of blacks from nearby Mississippi and Arkansas to pad ballot boxes. There was, no doubt, an element of truth in these beliefs, but many of the charges against the machine were exaggerated or false. The secret to Crump's control of Memphis was simple: efficiency. The organization knew its supporters, paid their poll taxes, and got them to the polls on election day. Blacks were indeed trucked to polling places but they were Memphians picked up at their work places. In the final analysis, Crump gave the Bluff City good services at low cost and bread and circuses and Memphians seemed to approve. Crump's candidate slates for both city and county offices invariably won by large majorities and the votes came from all ethnic groups and socioeconomic classes.

It is doubtful that the Memphis boss had an overpowering desire to become a dominant power in state politics. However, maintaining control in Memphis and Shelby County required it. Crump's ouster in 1915 as mayor was a painful reminder of what a rural legislature could do to an urban leader. More important, cities in Tennessee did not have complete home rule and effective operation of local communities required the passage by the General Assembly of numerous "local bills." Normally, local bills passed routinely but an urban leader submitting local measures could be weakened if a hostile legislature refused passage or a governor vetoed them. Moreover, state patronage and control of election machinery were in the hands of the governor. Denying both to Crump would be a severe blow to his status as political boss in Memphis. Finally, hostile attorney generals and grand juries could be a source of harassment. Thus it was vital that Crump have sufficient power in state government to assure at least a workable relationship with governors and legislatures to end threats to his machine. The Memphis boss was in a strong position in 1932. Such was his command of the franchise in Shelby County that, between 1928 and 1948, he could deliver more than ten percent of the total vote in statewide primaries. Indeed, in the gubernatorial primaries of 1936, 1938, and 1942, he delivered more than fifteen percent of the total vote. Any candidate for a statewide office had to be concerned with the voting block of Memphis and Shelby County.

Crump had a valuable ally in Senator McKellar. Astute and with a dominant personality, the senator had, by his third term, come to regard his seat as a personal possession. He worked hard to hold on to his office; he answered his mail and looked into every complaint or inquiry from his constituents, large or small. McKellar knew the value of patronage and he rewarded his supporters and he developed a loose organization across the state of federal job holders beholden to him. He was, by 1933, a power in the Senate; he was chairman of the Post Office Committee and second-ranking member of the Finance Committee, both rich in patronage. McKellar's power was further enhanced in 1933 with the advent of President Franklin Delano Roosevelt's New Deal, a program of relief and recovery from the Depression. The plethora of New Deal agencies created many jobs in Tennessee and, with a Democratic president in the White House for the first time since 1921, McKellar was able to obtain more plums for his state. Ironically, he was unable to control the patronage of the most important federal project in the state, the Tennessee Valley Authority. Still, as he gained power in Washington, his power in Tennessee increased. Always wary, McKellar realized that he also needed friends in state

government. He especially wanted friendly election commissioners. Thus, like Crump, McKellar had a vested interest in the oc-
cupant of the governor's office. In 1932, the Crump-McKellar
alliance moved to establish hegemony in Tennessee.

The Democratic gubernatorial primary of 1932 was a crucial
one. The contestants were two earlier contenders, Hill McAlister
and Lewis Pope, and former governor Malcolm Patterson. Mc-
Alister was endorsed by Crump, McKellar, and the Nashville machine. He was quickly branded as the candidate of urban bosses.
Ironically, Patterson was backed by Luke Lea, his implacable foe
earlier in the century. The endorsement, however, was of dubious
value. Many people could not forget that Patterson pardoned Duncan Cooper, one of the convicted killers of the martyred Carmack.
Pope drew some sympathy from former Peay backers, but because
he had no organized support, few gave him a chance. Yet, in the
bitter race in which tempers frequently flared, there was a move to
Pope. In an election marred by violence at several polling places and
numerous charges of ballot frauds, McAlister won with a plurality
of forty-one percent of the votes cast. Surprisingly, Pope came in a
close second, only three percent behind the victor, and Patterson
was a distant third. The poor showing of Patterson was indicative
of Lea's declining influence in the state. McAlister took more than
fifty percent of the large urban vote; Pope and Patterson split the
rural, small town, and small urban votes thus enabling the cities to
nominate the Democratic gubernatorial candidate for the first time.

Lewis Pope refused to accept defeat. He charged that he had
been denied victory by fraudulent ballots and the trucking of in-
eligible blacks to the polls in Memphis. He therefore declared as an
independent candidate in the general election. Mounting an intense attack and directing his fire on Crump, Pope caused concern
in the Democratic camp. Other things being equal, his candidacy
might have given hopes to Republicans but, because of internal divisions, the minority party was unable to take advantage of Democratic problems. McAlister won the governorship easily.
Republican candidate John T. McCall came in a respectable second
and Pope was a distant third. In the presidential race, the Democratic hopeful, Roosevelt, defeated the Republican hopeful by two
to one. Tennesseans were clearly ready for the presidency of a man

who promised relief from the Depression. The election of 1932 was
the beginning of a new era in Tennessee politics. Despite the continuing hostility between cities and country, an urban boss, Ed
Crump, and his ally Senator McKellar, put together an alliance of
petty fiefdoms across the state that was to dominate the Democratic
party and politics in Tennessee over the next eighteen years. The
coalition was, however, an uneasy one and the new governor in
1933, from Crump's point of view, proved to be an unhappy choice.

Governor McAlister's first priority when he became chief executive in 1933 was to dismantle the administrative reform of Governor Peay. One measure he succeeded in obtaining from the
General Assembly required State Senate confirmation of cabinet
appointments. Another act took the functions of budgeting and ac-
counting away from the administrative branch. These measures
weakened the power of the governor and strengthened the legislature. More important, McAlister was a weak administrator and
hesitant to take effective action on the state's pressing problems, especially declining revenue and a mounting state debt. The Memphis boss was annoyed at the governor's lack of aggressiveness and
doubtless would have preferred someone else to run for the nomination in 1934. He had no choice but to go along with McAlister.
The alternative in the primary was Lewis Pope, now an anathema
to Crump because of vicious attacks on the Memphis organization.
Pope carried on another virulent campaign but, with the two-term
tradition in his favor, McAlister won renomination by a large majority. Pope ran again as an independent but was no more successful than in 1932 and McAlister was reelected governor.

Two Senate posts were before the electorate in 1934. In a full-
term race, Senator McKellar proved once again his vote-getting
ability by winning both renomination and reelection over token
opposition. A short-term race was occasioned by Senator Cordell
Hull's resignation to join President Roosevelt's cabinet as secretary
of state. A Chattanooga jurist, Nathan Bachman, had been given
the interim appointment, and he became a candidate to complete
the remaining two years of the term. His opponent was Gordon
Browning, congressman from the eighth district. Bachman was
supported by Crump, McKellar, and the McAlister administration.
His organized support gave him the victory, but Browning ran a

respectable race. More important, Browning's campaign introduced to Tennesseans an exciting new personality.

A native of Carroll County in West Tennessee, Browning had served as a captain of an artillery company in World War I and was popular with his men. In 1922, he won the first of six consecutive terms in Congress. His record was undistinguished but he had a solid base of support among the veterans of the war. Browning was ambitious to move up to the Senate but circumstances limited him to challenging for only one seat. An unwritten but cardinal rule of Tennessee politics prohibited any of the three Grand Divisions from monopolizing the Senate posts. Tradition therefore dictated that, as a West Tennessean, Browning could only try for the seat occupied by McKellar who, it appeared, was unbeatable. His race against Bachman, an East Tennessean, violated tradition but there was calculation in Browning's effort. A long-standing practice in the Volunteer State was for aspirants to statewide offices make a perfunctory first, if futile, race in order to gain exposure and attract backers. Browning accomplished his goal. During the Senate contest in 1934, Tennesseans across the state grew acquainted with a charming, dynamic, and aggressive personality. He emerged from that race as the most available candidate for the governorship in 1936. Browning's long-term plan was to win the governorship in 1936, earn a second term, and then, with control of state patronage and the political machinery in the state, challenge McKellar in 1940. Early in 1936, he announced as a candidate for the Democratic gubernatorial nomination.

The dominant coalition had difficulty not only in agreeing on a candidate for governor but in finding a strong one. Crump had broken with McAlister when the governor had tried to push a sales tax through the General Assembly in 1935. He announced that he would probably sit out the gubernatorial contest. Not so with McKellar. He was aware of Browning's ambition and indeed feared that the former congressman would be a formidable foe in 1940. He therefore privately endorsed the McAlister administration's candidate, education commissioner, Burgin Dossett. In the canvass, Browning proved to be a natural campaigner. He mixed eloquence and humor in his speeches, charming audiences and reducing his opponents to humiliation with ridicule. Dossett, in

contrast, was colorless and humorless on the campaign trail. It soon
became apparent that Browning was the likely winner. Crump may
have had reservations about Browning, whose sympathies were
known to be with the countryside, but he had no desire to back a
loser. Late in the campaign, he announced his support for the former congressman. The endorsement revealed a rift between the
Memphis boss and McKellar. The wisdom of Crump's move was
demonstrated when the votes were counted. Browning won the
nomination by one of the widest margins and highest vote totals in
Tennessee history. Shelby County gave the victor just under 60,000
votes, but that was not decisive. Browning's margin was general
across the state and he went on to win the general election. He
earned the governor's office without the Memphis boss. The relationship between the new governor and Crump was harmonious
when Browning assumed his office in early 1937.

Few governors of Tennessee have had more success in the first
few months of an administration than Browning. The achievements during the regular session of the legislature were remark-
able. The first item of the agenda was another reorganization of
government along the lines of the 1923 plan. The result was both
greater efficiency and the strengthening of the power of the governor. Other reforms included implementation of the Federal Social Security program, increased appropriations for education, and
a tax package that increased revenue. By far the greatest achievement was reorganizing the state debt. At the onset of the Great
Depression, the Tennessee state debt amounted to $97,000,000 but
as revenue declined interest on the debt was financed with bonds.
By 1937, the debt had risen to almost $129,000,000. Browning se-
cured legislative authorization to fund the debt and a delegated tax
for payment of interest. Reorganization of the debt placed the state
on a sound financial basis and improved the state's credit. The governor was assisted in most of his reform agenda by the Shelby delegation in the General assembly but the honeymoon between
Crump and Browning was soon to end.

It was inevitable that Crump and Browning would part company. They were opposites. Crump was the Bourbon progressive
and the symbol of urban interests. Browning, raised in a populist
environment, represented the interests of rural and small-town

Tennessee. Both had dominant personalities and would not subordinate themselves to others. Moreover, the Memphis boss constituted a potential stumbling block to the governor's ambition. Cracks in the facade of harmony appeared when Crump expressed opposition to funding the state debt. The Memphis boss was upset in April 1937 when, upon the death of Nathan Bachman, the governor appointed a labor leader, George Leonard Berry as interim senator. Aware of the growing hostility, Browning concluded that he could not count on Crump as an ally in a reelection bid in 1938, much less his support in an effort to unseat McKellar in 1940. The aggressive and impetuous governor therefore decided to destroy the political power of the boss of the Bluff City.

In October 1937, Browning launched a sudden and massive attack on Crump and his organization. He publicly denounced the Memphis boss as head of a corrupt machine whose evil shadow was spreading across Tennessee. To prevent Crump from gaining control of the state, he called the legislature into special session and, using all the powers at his command, he rammed through the General Assembly two measures. One established a county unit voting system for statewide offices, an act that would place small counties on a par with the heavily populated urban counties. The second measure authorized the governor to conduct a purge of the voter registration books in Shelby County. A few weeks later, Browning convened the General Assembly again and the legislature created a commission to investigate alleged criminal activities in Memphis and strengthened the governor's control over the election machinery in the state. Browning hoped to mobilize support in the countryside for his attack on Crump, but he was only partially successful in this. Many of his own supporters regarded his measures as extreme if not undemocratic. The governor, in fact, polarized the state. Moreover, if there had been even the slightest rift in the relationship between Crump and McKellar, Browning's assault reunited them in a common cause: the defeat of the governor. The unit scheme was quickly challenged in the courts and, much to Browning's dismay, was overturned by the State Supreme Court in March 1938. Opposition to Browning, led by Crump and McKellar, gained momentum.

The first task was to find a candidate to challenge the governor for the Democratic nomination in 1938, but there were few available. Reluctantly, McKellar and Crump endorsed one announced candidate, the little-known state senator from Shelbyville, Prentice Cooper. At McKellar's behest, Crump endorsed Chancellor Tom Stewart of Winchester as a candidate for the Senate against George Berry. Stewart's chief claim to fame was as the attorney general of record in the Scopes trial in 1925. The Democratic primary in 1938 produced a rarity. Normally, candidates for statewide offices avoided coalitions as potentially more dangerous than rewarding. Cooper, Stewart, and William David Hudson, candidate for the Public Service Commission, however, united their efforts in a co-alition ticket. In contrast, Browning did not tie himself to Berry because the appointment had proved to be unpopular.

The Democratic primary campaign was one of the most hard-fought in the annals of Tennessee politics. It was not a spotless campaign as both sides used gutter tactics to gain advantages. McKellar's federal officeholders worked for the coalition and the vast state bureaucracy assisted Browning. Cooper carried on a rel-atively mild campaign, for it appeared that the real contest was be-tween Browning and the Memphis boss. Indeed, the governor focused most of his fire on Crump, insisting that the real issue was whether the people or a dictator should rule the state. The Mem-phis boss purchased full-page ads in the state's newspapers to vilify Browning.

There were a number of issues in the campaign for governor but the most important to the voters involved the measures of the special sessions. The question was whether the electorate should retain as governor a man who had sought to disfranchise thou-sands of voters. There were predictions of violence at polling places across the state but election day was relatively quiet. The voters spoke. Stewart won over Berry and Cooper gave Browning a re-sounding defeat. Shelby County alone gave Cooper nearly 58,000 votes. Ironically, Browning would have lost even if the unit system had been in effect.

With the defeat of Browning and Berry, the Crump-McKellar axis reached its peak of power in Tennessee. Senator Stewart, pliant and unobtrusive, was no threat to McKellar's dominant position as senior United States senator. Both Crump and McKellar had a friend in the governor's office and was therefore no threat to the hegemony of the Memphis boss in his own community. Governor Cooper was by no means a puppet, but such was the harmony within the dominant coalition that he won renomination and reelection in 1940 with ease and McKellar retained his seat against only token opposition. The Democratic primary two years later provided a scare for the ruling alliance. Governor Cooper announced for a third term and the lackluster Stewart entered the race for a full Senate term. Crump was no longer enthusiastic with either but McKellar persuaded the Memphis boss to support both. Cooper defeated Congressman John Ridley Mitchell narrowly outside of Shelby County, but 47,000 votes in Memphis gave him a comfortable margin. Stewart, who was challenged by Edward Ward Carmack, Jr., the son of the martyred editor, won only because of a heavy turnout in Memphis. Perhaps the only serious conflict between the governor and the Memphis boss involved the poll tax. Cooper sought repeal against the opposition of Crump, who used the tax to maintain voter turnout at a manageable level. The difference did not result in a break. The Crump-McKellar coalition seemed unbeatable in the 1940s and the opposition reached its nadir when Congressman Jim Nance McCord won the governorship in 1944 without opposition.

Many contemporaries and later interpreters concluded that Ed Crump was boss of Tennessee and that Senator McKellar was his lackey in Washington. The senator was definitely not a lackey nor even a lieutenant to the Memphis boss. They were friends, ideological allies, and had separate spheres of influence—McKellar a state organization and Crump a city machine. The two complemented rather than threatened each other. When they cooperated, they were unbeatable. Ed Crump was not boss of Tennessee. He exercised power at the state level primarily to protect his own bailiwick. In the late 1930s, he could deliver close to 60,000 votes to the candidate of his choice in statewide elections, easily enough to determine the outcome in a close race. He was without doubt the single most powerful political leader in Tennessee between 1932 and 1948 and any aspirant to state office had to be concerned with the Memphis boss. According to conventional wisdom, the Democratic party contained two factions: Crump and anti-Crump. In reality, Tennessee's Democracy remained an amorphous collection of factions, feudal baronies, and petty fiefdoms. Many local and regional leaders, both urban and rural, found it desirable to cooperate with Crump and McKellar for logrolling and trading of favors in the legislature. According to legend, East Tennessee Republican bosses received favors and patronage for not challenging the dominant Democratic coalition. Local and regional bosses were not under Crump's thumb. Nevertheless, the coalition, with the Memphis boss and McKellar as the most powerful leaders, became one of the most powerful alliance systems in Tennessee's history.

If Crump had tried to become a state boss in the strict sense, the attempt would have failed. The astute leader of Memphis must have realized that goal was beyond his reach. Rural Tennesseans would not have tolerated rule by a city boss. At no time during the years of his power did Crump make an attempt to change Tennessee's fundamental law to give cities home rule. Neither did he press for reapportionment to strengthen urban representation in the legislature. The Memphis boss scrupulously avoided rocking the boat. In a very real sense, he achieved at least a temporary rapprochement between city and country by not muddying the waters. The countryside thus retained the upper hand in the General Assembly and was ever on guard against threats to rural hegemony.

The years from the early 1920s to the mid-1940s were years of intense political conflict in Tennessee. Historically, this was the norm. There was, however, an underlying ideological continuity or what George Brown Tindall calls a "persistent tradition of community." During the progressive era, those of the conservative Bourbon persuasion adjusted to the demands of reform and became the business progressives of the new era. The administration of Governor Peay reflected the reconciliation of tradition with innovation. He addressed the issues of efficiency in government and expanded services but went no further with reform. The rise of Luke Lea wrought no ideological departure. Governor Browning was, in a sense, an anomaly. Although by no means a liberal, he was a latter-day populist and the spokesman for the small farmer. Ed Crump and Kenneth McKellar epitomized the reconciliation of tradition with reform. Both came from the landed aristocracy but made the transition to business progressivism. Beyond that, both were conservative, conscious of class, had a paternalistic attitude toward society, and sought to maintain the traditions of the Old South. Although politically stronger, their regime was almost identical to the Bourbon regulars of the latter nineteenth century in Tennessee. After 1945, the dominant ideological persuasion was confronted by a new threat.

Chapter 5

The Bulldozer Revolution

At the end of World War II in 1945, the Volunteer State was at the threshold of revival of economic growth. The industrialization and urbanization that had begun after the Civil War and accelerated during the progressive era and in the 1920s was abruptly halted in 1929 with the onset of the Great Depression. The first to feel the impact of the economic downturn were the industrial workers. As production slowed, those in manufacturing were laid off in increasing numbers and by 1933, one third of the state's industries had closed. Unemployment was rife and increasing bank and business failures made matters worse. Because agriculture had experienced depression throughout the 1920s, farmers did not immediately feel the effects of the slump, but by 1933 farm prices had fallen sharply and hard times were felt in the country.

The election of Franklin D. Roosevelt to the presidency in 1932 and the advent of the New Deal provided some measure of relief to Tennesseans. The various agencies and farm programs of the New Deal spent money and provided jobs in the state but the efforts served only as a palliative rather than a cure for the economic ills in the Volunteer State. By far the most significant New Deal contribution to the state's economy was the Tennessee Valley Authority, a regional redevelopment program enacted by Congress in

1933. Under TVA, a series of dams on the Tennessee River was built to improve river navigation and provide hydroelectricity to Tennessee and adjacent states. TVA also had the mandate of assisting in reclamation and reforestation of millions of acres of worn-out lands. The redevelopment agency accomplished its goals in the long run; more immediately, the building of dams, power plants, and transmission lines provided jobs, thus stimulating the economy. There were signs of economic revival in the state before the decade of the 1930s closed but it was World War II that produced recovery from the Depression. The war caused an economic boom in the Volunteer State. Senator McKellar, because of his seniority in the Senate, procured for the state a number of military bases and support facilities. Many existing industries turned to producing war materials full time and because of the availability of cheap hydroelectricity, a number of war production industries located in Tennessee. Employment was high and there was a renewed migration to the cities. When the war ended, and the predicted depression failed to materialize, old and new industries converted to consumer production and Tennessee entered a period of rapid economic growth and change.

Between 1945 and 1965, the number of manufacturing establishments in Tennessee more than doubled, creating thousands of wage-paying jobs. The new industries were diversified and included chemicals, lumber and timber by-products, and textiles. East Tennessee remained the leader in industry but there was significant growth in the middle section. Farming also underwent a revolution. Success in conservation, reclamation, and reforestation had beneficial effects on agriculture. Mechanization reduced the need for farm labor and the number of farmers and farms declined. Yet the acreage per farm increased and, with the application of scientific methods, production increased sharply. Agriculture also diversified. Cotton, for example, declined in importance as other crops such as soybeans increased, as did dairying and livestock farming. Industrialization and changes in agriculture accelerated the migration from the countryside to the cities.

In the quarter of a century from the beginning of World War II, the demography of Tennessee was dramatically altered. Many rural counties declined in population while all cities grew rapidly, especially Memphis, which increased in population by more than thirty percent. One city that had not existed prior to the war, Oak Ridge, boasted of a population of more than 27,000. Such was the growth of cities that, by 1965, nearly sixty percent of the state's population was classified as urban and just over forty percent remained rural and small town. The figures had been just the opposite thirty years earlier. But there was another migratory pattern: a move from the central cities to the suburbs. On the fringes of all urban areas, bulldozers reshaped the landscape for housing developments and suburban shopping centers. Thus within less than a generation after World War II, the Volunteer State had made the transition from a predominantly rural and agrarian state to an urban and industrial one. The state's political institution, however, had difficulty in coping with the problems arising from rapid economic change.

At the end of the war, Tennessee did not have the resources to provide the services required in an expanding economy. Cities did not have the funds to build new or maintain old streets, much less expand other services. Rural roads were inadequate and the state's schools were in woeful condition. Although Governor McCord demonstrated courage by persuading the General Assembly in 1947 to enact a two percent sales tax to benefit education, the conservative Bourbon establishment dominating Tennessee politics seemed unwilling to address the problems of the industrial age. Ed Crump was getting old and perhaps out of touch with the times. Although reelected easily in 1946, the infirmities of age made Senator McKellar ineffective as a political leader. Tennesseans were restive because of the inertia of the conservative establishment. An emerging middle class and youthful business and professional leaders, anxious for a better climate for economic growth, regarded passive, inactive government as inadequate for the times. Organized labor was beginning to assert itself. Finally, returning veterans found the internal paths to power clogged by the vested interests within the establishment. The mood in the immediate postwar years in the Volunteer State was for political change and focused on the issue of "bossism."

Machine rule was, to a greater or lesser degree, widespread in Tennessee. Machines—urban, small town, and rural—ranged from

well-knit organizations to authoritarian rule. Reinforcing the belief
that the state was dominated by bosses was the opinion of many
contemporaries that the boss of Memphis, had in fact, become boss
of the state. Increasingly in the postwar years, Tennesseans came
to view machine rule as antidemocratic and an impediment to progress. A vocal and militant minority equated boss rule with dictatorship. The nation had recently fought a war against dictators
abroad; now it was time to end dictatorship and restore democracy
at home. In 1946, for example, veterans in two East Tennessee
counties, Polk and McMinn, donned combat boots, armed themselves, and used force to oust local bosses. At the state level, a crusade against Crump was well under way before the war ended.

Opposition to Crump in Memphis had never been entirely ab-
sent. One of his most severe critics had been Edward John Meeman, editor of the evening *Press Scimitar* who, through his editorials,
became something of a gadfly to Crump. Meeman, however, failed
to arouse Memphians to defeat the machine. More successful in the
long run was the *Nashville Tennessean*. Published by New Deal liberal Silliman Evans, the newspaper had the largest circulation within
Tennessee and was especially influential in the mid-state area. Early
in the 1940s, and perhaps motivated by a desire to become one of
the political power brokers in the Democratic party, Evans set
Crump as an issue on the social agenda. Editorially, the *Tennessean*
kept repeating the charge that Crump was not only the head of a
corrupt city machine but exercised evil influence in state government. The campaign paid no dividends in 1944 when the candidate endorsed by the Memphis boss won the governorship
uncontested. In 1946, however, the *Tennessean's* crusade began to
bear fruit.

In 1946, when no one stepped forward to challenge the Crump-
backed McCord in the Democratic primary for governor, a group
of dissidents qualified Gordon Browning. The *Tennessean* quickly
boarded the bandwagon. Despite his overwhelming defeat in 1938,
Browning remained personally popular and was the best known
anti-Crump politician in the state. He also had regained public es-
teem by service in World War II and at the time he was qualified,
was a colonel in the military government in Germany. Although he
refused to leave his post, he allowed his name to remain in the race

and his "friends" to campaign for him. The results were gratifying. McCord won as expected but the candidate in absentia polled almost forty percent of the vote. Browning emerged as the leading contender for the Democratic gubernatorial nomination in 1948.

The Democratic primaries of 1948 were the hardest fought in a decade and proved to be a watershed in Tennessee politics. Governor McCord, with Crump's blessing, announced for a third term. He had two handicaps aside from the third-term issue: he had sponsored the unpopular sales tax and had alienated organized labor by backing and signing a state right-to-work law. As expected, Browning entered the governor's race. The senatorial contest was a three-way affair. Senator Stewart announced for renomination, but Crump, who had long since lost confidence in the lackluster solon, backed another contender, Judge John Mitchell of Cookeville. Another candidate was Congressman Estes Kefauver of Chattanooga. Kefauver was regarded as a liberal although the reputation was not entirely earned. In any case, he was charismatic and won the confidence of business and professional leaders in the urban centers, especially Memphis. Browning and Kefauver were endorsed by Evans's *Tennessean* and both made bossism and Ed Crump the chief issue. Although the two candidates did not form a coalition, their attacks on the Memphis boss made it appear that theirs was a joint effort. Indeed, Browning helped Kefauver in rural areas while the latter boosted the gubernatorial candidate's stock in the cities. Crump, as was his custom, purchased full-page ads in the state's newspapers to castigate his opponents. On one occasion, he likened Kefauver to a pet coon that tried to deceive by stealing while looking in another direction. The senatorial candidate responded that he was certainly not Crump's pet coon and began wearing a coonskin cap as his symbol. When the votes were counted, Browning had won with about fifty-six percent of the votes. McCord carried Shelby County, but the challenger polled a surprising 20,000 votes in Memphis. Kefauver won a plurality with forty-four percent of the vote in the senatorial primary. Mitchell, Crump's candidate, came in a poor third. The Memphis boss blundered by ditching Stewart. The votes for Mitchell could have been the difference between defeat and victory for Stewart.

For the first time in almost a generation, the Republican party came alive in 1948. Country music entertainer and star of the Grand Ole Opry Roy Acuff received the Republican nomination for governor and Congressman Brizilla Carroll Reece from the first district was the senatorial candidate. The Democratic nominees were concerned with the threat but both won easily in the general election. The presidential election of that year, however, provided a clue to a future trend in Tennessee politics. Harry S Truman, who succeeded to the presidency upon Roosevelt's death in 1945 and who sought to carry forward the New Deal, was the Democratic nominee. Republicans had high hopes for victory for the national Democracy was rent with dissension. Ultraliberals put forth a candidate and because the Democratic platform called for civil rights legislation, some Southerners bolted, formed the Dixiecrat party, and placed a candidate on the ballot. The Dixiecrats ran well in Tennessee and Truman, the ultimate victor, barely carried the state. It was sixteen years before another Democratic presidential candidate would win the Volunteer State.

The single most important result of the elections of 1948 was the collapse of the Crump-McKellar axis. Yet despite defections in his home community, the Memphis boss remained strong in the Bluff City and he still had some influence at the state level. Mc-Kellar remained a power in the Senate but because of his age, he was ineffective and no longer controlled his organization in Tennessee. Indeed, some members were already looking for another place to land. The alliance system that dominated the state after the elections was weak and unstable. Browning was the titular head of the Democratic party and controlled party machinery, but members of his organization regarded Kefauver and his followers with some disdain. The latter's loyalists could not, with some justification, bring themselves to trust the Browning crowd. The governor was unable, if not unwilling, to use his patronage power in a ruthless manner to build a strong organization. He was also an anomaly. Browning, whose rural bias was well known, was elected governor at a time when rapid growth required increased attention to the needs of the cities. As the best-known anti-Crump politico, he was at the right place at the right time to reclaim the governor-

ship. Still, he encountered no serious difficulties in his first legislative session in 1949.

Governor Browning's legislative program was a success by any
measure. At his request, the General Assembly enacted a long list
of election reforms, including the virtual end of the poll tax, the
permanent registration of voters in larger communities, the use of
metal ballot boxes where voting machines were not used, and a requirement that all election board meetings be open to the public.
The legislature also increased appropriations for education. The
governor's pet measure provided for the construction of hard-sur-
faced roads in rural Tennessee, a measure that drew praise in the
countryside. The major controversy involved a proposal by the
state's trucking industry that weights allowed on the state's highways be increased. The measure was rejected only because Browning put pressure on the legislature. Yet the governor's hold on the
Democratic party was tenuous, which was demonstrated in the gubernatorial primary in 1950. He was expecting an easy race, for his
only opponent was State Senator Clifford Allen of Nashville who
was, apparently, looking to the future and making his first obligatory statewide campaign. The little-known Allen gave Browning a
scare by polling about forty-three percent of the vote. The governor had no problem in the general election, however. For the first
time in its history in Tennessee, the Republican party failed to put
up a candidate for governor. The legislative session of 1951 was de-
void of controversy and relatively quiet.

One of Browning's liabilities was that he had offended an increasingly powerful lobby for urban interests, the Tennessee Municipal League. During the legislative session in 1949, the League
had extracted a pledge from the governor to support a return of a
portion of the state gasoline tax to the cities for street construction
and repair. When it became apparent that the money would be
needed for his rural roads program, Browning reneged. The Municipal League then became a dangerous enemy and would play an
important role in the election of 1952.

The Democratic statewide primaries in 1952 were crucial. In
addition to the biennial governor's race, Senator McKellar's seat was
before the electorate. The eighty-three-year-old and frequently ill
senator refused to retire and declared as a candidate. For the first

time since his initial election to the Senate, McKellar appeared vulnerable to defeat. It was therefore Browning's best opportunity to win the office he so coveted. Unfortunately, the youthful and aggressive Congressman Albert Gore preempted the governor by securing sufficient commitments of support, many from Browning's friends, for the Senate race. The disappointed governor then declared for a third term. Clifford Allen also entered the gubernatorial contest, but a third candidate and the one who ultimately became Browning's main challenger provided an interesting departure from tradition. Normally an aspirant to the governorship first served in one or more lesser offices and then made an obligatory race to gain recognition before making a serious bid. Thirty-two-year-old Frank Goad Clement, the scion of a politically active family from Dickson, had little political experience and had held no elective office when he announced for governor. But a number of astute and experienced political professionals and some rising young leaders quickly perceived that he had potential and boarded Clement's bandwagon. Clement had a strange quality of glamour. He was articulate, eloquent, and charismatic on the speaker's platform. Sometimes he became emotional and, quoting Scriptures, his political speeches often sounded like sermons. Frequently, he closed with the expression, "precious Lord, take my hand, lead me on." During the summer months, he wore a white linen suit, projecting an image of purity and honesty. Clement quickly replaced Allen as Browning's chief opponent.

Frank Clement's efforts in 1952 might well have remained a trial run had not Browning blundered. First, he committed the state to a lease-purchase of the Memorial Apartments, a building in downtown Nashville for use as state office space. There was apparently nothing corrupt about the deal, but it was not a wise political move for it was charged that some close friends and contributors to the governor's campaign would profit handsomely. The deal reinforced charges that the Browning administration was guilty of cronyism, favoritism in awarding contracts, and waste and inefficiency in general. The second error was an overcommitment to the support of Senator Kefauver's bid for the Democratic presidential nomination in 1952. After winning some fame in televised hearings on organized crime, Kefauver announced for the presidency, entered and won a number of preferential primaries, and went to the convention with a substantial lead in delegate votes. At the convention, at Kefauver's request, the Tennessee delegation voted against seating the Virginia delegation for refusing to pledge support to the party's nominee. The vote against a sister Southern state caused a wave of fury to spread across the Volunteer State and, because he was the chairman of the delegation, much of the anger was focused on Browning. As the gubernatorial campaign closed, Clement was on the offensive on issues such as general corruption, the Memorial Apartments transaction, and humiliation at the Democratic convention and Browning was on the defensive.

The Senate race was comparatively quiet. McKellar was so feeble that he was unable to make more than one or two appearances. Gore campaigned vigorously but he refused to criticize the aging incumbent; rather, he emphasized that it was time for a younger man. The campaign of 1952 affords an example of the lack of cohesiveness among the factions within the Democratic party. Individuals in the camps of both Browning and Clement divided their support for the senatorial aspirants. The senatorial race was never in doubt. Gore won by a large majority. Clement also won a plurality and about forty-nine percent of the vote; Browning was well back with only thirty-nine percent. The results of the 1952 primary were as much a change of the guard as the one four years earlier.

Frank Clement emerged from the primary as a powerful figure in the Democratic party. He forged a coalition that dominated Tennessee politics for almost twenty years. Although remnant factions of the old Crump-McKellar axis were welcomed into Clement's alliance system, it was not, as some charged, a revival of the old machine. The leadership was clearly different and the locus of power shifted away from Memphis to Nashville. At the same time, both Senators Gore and Kefauver had separate alliance systems that were based on federal patronage and personal friendships. Clement's, because he controlled state patronage and election machinery, was more cohesive and stronger. The forces of the two senators were reasonably cooperative but there existed some enmity between the governor and Kefauver. The latter feared, with some justification, that Clement coveted his Senate seat.

Clement's command of the political scene was evident when the General Assembly met in 1953. At his request, the legislature redeemed a pledge he had made to the Tennessee Municipal League to return more state revenue to the cities. There were increased appropriations for education and standardized purchasing procedures were adopted. In addition, the General Assembly created a mental health department, a measure dear to Clement's heart. The governor believed his most significant achievements were in the area of improved treatment of mental illness. A scandal broke after the legislature increased truck weights on Tennessee's highways. It was then revealed that the trucking industry had contributed heavily to Clement's campaign. More important than the governor's legislative program was the convening of a constitutional convention in 1953, the first since the fundamental law was established in 1870. The convention proposed two amendments to the constitution. One provided home rule for cities, thus removing the cities from control by the General Assembly. The only major concern of urban centers remaining now was unequal representation in the legislature and that would be rectified a decade later. Another amendment extended the governor's term by two years, beginning in 1955. After perhaps toying with the idea of running against Kefauver for the Democratic senatorial nomination, Clement announced as a candidate for the first four-year term.

The Democratic gubernatorial primary of 1954 was almost a repeat of the one two years earlier. Bitter over insinuations that he had been dishonest and seeking vindication, Gordon Browning, against advice from friends, entered the race against Clement. He sought to raise the old Crump bugbear and charged that Clement's administration was a revival of control of the state by the old Memphis machine. Clement remained aloof of the charge and carried on a positive campaign, emphasizing his achievements. A new issue—school desegregation—was injected into the race. In May of that year, the United States Supreme Court declared racial segregation in the nation's schools unconstitutional. Near the end of the campaign, Browning declared that if elected governor, he would resist integration in the state. Clement avoided extreme rhetoric but stated that the decision was the law of the land. The senatorial race that year involved the seat occupied by Kefauver. His rival was archconservative Pat Sutton, the sixth district congressman from Lawrenceburg. Sutton conducted an innovative campaign, traveling about in a helicopter and appearing on television "talkathons." He was vicious in his attacks on Kefauver and charged that the senator was "soft on communism." Regarding Sutton's anticommunist pitch as a serious threat, Kefauver campaigned vigorously but his concern was exaggerated for he defeated his opponent by a two-to-one margin. In the governor's race, to no one's surprise, Clement polled 440,000 votes to Browning's humiliating 186,000. The incumbent carried every county in the state except Browning's home county, Carroll. The vote was an indication of the young governor's popularity and power in Tennessee.

Clement's four-year term was generally calm and uneventful. The governor's legislative program was modestly progressive and successful. Except for the question of school desegregation and a few problems the agile Clement was able to sidestep, no major issue disturbed political serenity in the Volunteer State. The popular young governor also succeeded in cultivating a positive reputation beyond Tennessee, for he had aspirations for national office. Indeed, he had a plan. First, he would secure the coveted honor of giving the keynote address at the Democratic National Convention in 1956. He would so impress the convention with his forensic talents that he would be made the vice-presidential candidate. The Democratic ticket that year was not expected to win but the exposure would enable Clement to become the front-runner for the presidential nomination in 1960. He was awarded the keynote address but his plans went awry beyond that. Clement was a spellbinder but his effort at the convention was bombastic and he failed to generate enthusiasm. He was not considered when it came time to nominate a vice-presidential candidate. Instead, Senator Kefauver, who had once again tried for the presidential nomination but had lost to Adlai Stevenson at the convention, was a contender. So also was Senator Gore, who had earned a good reputation in the Senate. Kefauver won second place on the national ticket largely because he was popular among Democrats at the grass roots across the nation.

Despite the failure of his plans at the convention, Clement remained strong in Tennessee and his coalition the dominant political force in the state. There was occasional discord and defections. Such was the strength of the coalition that, at the end of the four-year term and unable to succeed himself, Clement could name the alliance's candidate for the Democratic nomination for governor in 1958, Buford Ellington. Although born in Mississippi, Ellington had moved to Tennessee and settled in Marshall County. He was Clement's state campaign manager in 1952 and then became commissioner of the Department of Agriculture. Although a few defected, most of the factions in Clement's coalition endorsed him. Initially, there were a number of trial balloons lofted, but most pulled down before the campaign began. Even so, the field was crowded. Candidates included Memphis mayor Edmund Orgill, who had the background support of Kefauver and part of his organization; Judge Andrew "Tip" Taylor of Jackson, a scion of Tennessee's famous Taylor family; and Clifford Allen made another race. There were relatively few issues in the campaign and it was hard to find differences between the candidates except on the race question. Taylor was an avowed segregationist. Ellington believed in segregation of the races but tempered his stand, as did Orgill, to avoid alienating too many voters.

When the ballots had been counted, Ellington won with a plurality and 213,000 votes, but Orgill was only 8,000 behind in second, and Taylor was third with only 300 less than Orgill. Allen was a distant fourth. The victor's votes came largely from rural Middle and East Tennessee; Orgill's were urban; and Taylor won most of West Tennessee. Had only a handful of votes changed, the outcome of the primary would have been different. Lee Greene, Clement's biographer, argues that Ellington would have won in a head-to-head contest with any of the three. At any rate, the very closeness of the outcome almost precluded an independent in the general election. Thus the aging former governor, Jim McCord, qualified but few leaders in the Democratic party were willing to desert the party's nominee. Ellington defeated the independent and the little-known Republican candidate, Thomas Wall, easily in the general election. In the senatorial primary, Albert Gore defeated his challenger, former governor Prentice Cooper, by a comfortable margin and then trounced his Republican opponent in the general election.

In January 1959, Clement was out of office for the first time in six years. The still young, consummate politician was soon restless and he gave some thought to challenging Senator Kefauver in 1960. Why he failed to run is not clear. Very likely he realized that it would be difficult if not impossible to defeat the incumbent, something Andrew Taylor discovered. Taylor ran against Kefauver in the Democratic primary and tried to portray the senator as not representative of the majority of Tennesseans. Kefauver turned back Taylor by a vote of two to one and had no difficulty in winning the general election. Clement's problem was that Ellington now controlled the well-oiled machine that he had put together. Moreover, differences that were both serious and trivial as well as personal and ideological strained their relationship. Ellington was deeply conservative, and opposing activist government, he offered no new programs. Yet he maintained programs inaugurated under Clement without the need to increase revenue. Ellington was, of course, unable to succeed himself, and as his term neared the end, it was obvious that Clement was anxious to return to the governor's office. Governor Ellington no doubt wanted to block Clement's efforts and perhaps he tried. Despite his control of the machine, the governor was unable to prevent the charismatic former governor from obtaining commitments of support from most of the factions in the coalition.

The Democratic primary in 1962 attracted a number of hopefuls but, unable to secure the necessary commitments, most withdrew. Only three remained. Clement, with the old coalition behind him, was the leader. Another candidate was a former Clement supporter, Chattanooga mayor Rudy Olgiati. A third contender was William W. Farris, public works commissioner for the city of Memphis. The race was an unexciting affair. Both Olgiati and Farris apparently realized that Clement was the man to beat and focused their attacks on the leader, emphasizing his connection with a political machine. There were efforts, particularly by the *Tennessean,* to get one of the two to withdraw because Clement was almost certain to win with both in the race. Both refused to pull out. Clement won the primary with forty-two percent of the vote; Olgiati was second with twenty-nine percent and Farris third with twenty-eight. The victor had won with a plurality and not a clear mandate.

Whether either Olgiati or Farris alone could have beaten Clement cannot be known. Considering that both had liabilities, it is doubtful that either could have defeated the popular former governor.

As in 1958, an independent entered the governor's race in the general election. But this time, the candidate, William Anderson, a retired navy commander and a genuine hero, was a greater threat than McCord had been four years earlier. Anderson had commanded the nuclear submarine, the *Nautilus,* on its historic voyage under the arctic ice cap and the North Pole in 1957. Anderson attacked the Democratic candidate and his machine and no doubt attracted the sizable anti-Clement vote. He polled 203,000 votes, far more than McCord did in 1958. Clement won with 315,000, but an unknown Republican received 100,000 votes. The victor's margin was not a comfortable one. According to Clement's biographer, this, with his minority win in the primary, suggests that the governor's popularity was beginning to wear thin. Nevertheless, Clement's new administration picked up in 1963 where he left off in 1958. He expanded programs such as mental health and pressed for significant increases in appropriations for education. This required more revenue and the sales tax was broadened, a move that did not have widespread approval. There was one vital issue that had been simmering for years: the question of apportionment. Although he had no direct responsibility, Clement had successfully evaded the problem in his first four-year term by failing to exercise leadership. The governor and the entire political establishment had no choice now but to try to deal with the problem.

Tennessee's constitution of 1870 required decennial reapportionment of the General Assembly. But on only one occasion, 1901, had representation been revised. Since that time, cities had increased in population enormously while the countryside declined. The result was that many rural counties had become, in effect, "rotten boroughs" while urban areas were grossly underrepresented. Rural Tennessee simply elected more representatives than the majority who lived in urban areas. Moreover, Republicans in East Tennessee were underrepresented. The problem for the cities was simple: urban areas were the major source of revenue but received a disproportionate share of appropriations. Rural legislators, protecting their monopoly, invariably and easily blocked attempts at reapportionment and it was an exercise in futility to propose changes in representation. Yet it may be argued that cities did not move aggressively to rectify the inequities because they were not truly urban in culture. Tennessee's cities were peopled by rural migrants and, as Michael J. McDonald and William Bruce Wheeler in a study of Knoxville suggest, while urban living required some adaptation, the migrants retained many of their rural beliefs, values, and norms. In a very real sense, cities in the Volunteer State were little more than overgrown small towns whose residents were sympathetic to the problems of the countryside. Nevertheless, by the 1950s, the inequity in malapportionment had become serious and proponents of reapportionment turned to the courts for relief.

In 1959, a class action suit, *Baker v. Carr,* was initiated requesting that the federal courts intervene and remedy malapportionment. A three-judge panel dismissed the case, citing lack of jurisdiction. However, on appeal, the Supreme Court of the United States agreed to hear the case. In 1962, the Supreme Court handed down a landmark decision, declaring that malapportioned legislatures were unconstitutional and remanded the case to district courts for remedy. A district court therefore mandated that both houses of the Tennessee General Assembly be reapportioned according to the principle of "one man, one vote." Unfortunately, the politicians in the Volunteer State had difficulty in conforming to the guidelines. Governor Ellington called the General Assembly into special session in 1962 to reapportion but the plan for the upper house was rejected by the court. Regular sessions in 1963 and 1965 were unable to please the federal judiciary. A constitutional convention that convened in 1965, in addition to providing for annual sessions of the General Assembly, adopted an amendment conforming to the mandate of the courts. Even so, the legislature of 1967 failed to develop a satisfactory plan. Finally, in 1968, a federal district court arbitrarily drew the State Senate district lines and a major political milestone and reform had been achieved. Immediately, the four metropolitan areas, Chattanooga, Knoxville, Nashville, and Memphis gained forty percent of the representation in the General Assembly and, combined with the smaller cities, urban Tennessee had in fact a working majority in the legislature. Almost simultaneously, another reform movement seemed to reach fruition.

The civil rights movement to end racial segregation in the South, a drive now referred to as the Second Reconstruction, wrought changes in races relations in Tennessee. Although the movement had been gaining momentum and minor victories had been won in the courts, the Supreme Court's decision in 1954 in the case of *Brown v. Board of Education, Topeka,* outlawing segregation in public schools, came as a shock to most white Tennesseans. As might be expected, there was some resistance. In areas of heavy black population, there was a revival of the Ku Klux Klan activity and, as in the deep South, white citizens councils were organized to resist school integration. There were ugly incidents and a riot occurred in 1956 when the school at Clinton was opened to blacks. Generally, however, in its tradition of moderation in racial matters, Tennessee accepted the Court's decision as the "law of the land." Both senators, Gore and Kefauver, refused to sign the "Southern Manifesto," a resolution by Southern members of Congress protesting the Court's decision. Governor Clement called out the National Guard to put down the riot and insure integration of the Clinton school. Except for one measure which Governor Clement vetoed, the General Assembly seemed reluctant to promote schemes to by-pass integration. This does not mean that white Tennesseans welcomed desegregation. Indeed, it is probable that a majority disapproved and accepted school integration only grudgingly. There was a proliferation of private schools for whites in the years after 1954 and Tennesseans were slow to integrate despite the Supreme Court's call for "all deliberate speed."

Other areas of the civil rights movement were met with relatively little resistance. After a series of "sit-in" demonstrations in Nashville in 1960, the downtown lunch counters were integrated. It is probable that the merchants in that city were motivated less by justice than by pragmatic economics. There was little overt protest in Tennessee to a series of civil rights measures passed by Congress in the mid-1960s, the Civil Rights Act of 1964, the Voting Rights Act of 1965, and open housing legislation. Significantly, a black from Memphis, A. W. Willis, was elected to the General Assembly in 1964. Thus, by the mid-1960s, blacks in the Volunteer State were on the verge of entering the cultural mainstream and participating actively in the social, political, and economic life of the state.

By avoiding the "massive resistance" to the Second Reconstruction by the deep Southern states, Tennessee earned a reputation as a moderate state with moderate if not liberal leadership. The nation's media and contemporary observers portrayed the state's leaders, Gore, Kefauver, and Clement, as progressive. There was substance to this image. Gore and Kefauver avoided racist rhetoric and refused to sign the "Southern Manifesto," thus provoking the wrath of conservatives across the South. The voting records of both in Congress tended toward the liberal side. Clement, by calling out the National Guard to enforce integration at Clinton provided sharp contrast to Governor Orval Faubus who used the guard to block desegregation in Little Rock, Arkansas. Moreover, Clement pressed genuine progressive measures. It should be noted that Tennessee's three talented politicians cultivated moderate images, for all had ambitions for national office. They realized that, as Southerners, a more liberal posture was necessary for acceptance beyond the South. It was an anomaly that a conservative state such as Tennessee retained in office three leaders with liberal images. Part of the answer lies in the fact that all were personally popular. More important, they were sustained in positions of responsibility by the pervasive New Deal coalition.

President Roosevelt's New Deal wrought a critical voter realignment in the South and Tennessee after 1933. The president in fact forged a coalition within the Democratic party of disparate elements, small farmers, urban ethnic groups, organized labor, blacks, and liberal intellectuals. The first to board the New Deal bandwagon in Tennessee were the Bourbon progressives such as Crump and McKellar, but by the end of the war, Roosevelt's emphasis on reform and providing benefits to the masses had alienated economic conservatives. Even so, the New Deal coalition emerged in the postwar years as the dominant voting force in the Volunteer State. The sentiment of the constituent voting blocks was for reform. It was this mood that brought about the downfall of bossism in Tennessee in 1948 and swept first Kefauver, and then Gore into office four years later. It was the New Deal coalition that helped Kefauver and Gore beat back challengers who used anticommunist and racist rhetoric and also sustained Clement in the governorship. But the liberalism in the Volunteer State should not be exaggerated.

Liberalism is relative and therefore difficult to measure. Certainly, by Tennessee standards, the two United States senators from the Volunteer State were liberal, but only moderate progressives at best when measured by standards beyond the South. The voting records in Congress of Gore and Kefauver were by no means extreme or radical; rather, they voiced concerns not unlike those of the populists and progressives of earlier generations. Clement's reforms were in response to constituent demands for more and better services. In a very real sense, the policies and achievements of the talented trio provide another example of the reconciliation of innovation with tradition. In spite of the New Deal coalition, traditional political patterns remained essentially unchanged.

The long-standing emphasis on localism, personality of candidates, and loose alliance systems remained the pattern in the post-World War II years. Political leaders had their own personal following and power was achieved by forging coalitions. Gore and Kefauver had their own separate, loosely knit organizations. Some contemporary observers argued, perhaps correctly, that rural and small-town satrapies were less powerful in the generation after the war. Nevertheless, it was from the small organizations that Clement put together an alliance system that dominated Tennessee politics for almost twenty years. Many members of the governor's coalition were conservative and his most ardent press supporter was the *Nashville Banner,* published by an arrant conservative, James Geddes Stahlman. Moreover, Clement's successor as governor as well as leader of the coalition was conservative Buford Ellington. The Clement-Ellington alliance system was as strong as the old Crump-McKellar axis. The strength of the system was demonstrated when Clement regained the governor's office in 1962 and then Ellington was elected again in 1966. Pundits dubbed their regime "leap frog" government. It has been suggested that Clement was the innovator and Ellington the consolidator, but by Ellington's second term, the coalition had begun to lose its control of the

Democratic party and Tennessee politics. By the mid-1960s, the twin trends of industrialization and urbanization and the issues of reapportionment and the Second Reconstruction converged to break up the Clement-Ellington machine and to destroy the New Deal voting coalition. In addition, the Republican party in Tennessee aroused from its long, deep slumber.

Chapter 6

A Two-Party State?

The Republicans remained the dominant party in the mountains and valleys of East Tennessee and in a few West Tennessee counties in the post-World War II years. The Grand Old Party was still a minority numerically but strong enough to threaten the Democratic party's control of the state. Like the Democracy, however, Republicans were riven by factionalism and internal quarrels. Early in the century, two groups, the "Black and Tans" and "Lily Whites," fought for control of the party. Urban blacks were an integral part of the former and an important block in the Republican vote across the state. In Memphis, Robert R. Church, Jr. put together a strong black organization and ultimately became a power in the Republican party. The "Black and Tans," led by J. Will Taylor and Church, won control of the party and when Republicans occupied the White House, dispensed federal patronage in Tennessee. The black Republican vote in Memphis began to decline as Boss Crump, dispensing favors, absorbed Negroes into his organization. Subsequently, Franklin D. Roosevelt succeeded in transferring the allegiance of blacks from the Republicans to the Democrats as part of the New Deal coalition. As a result of the rift between the "Black and Tans" and "Lily Whites," the Republican party became almost dormant in contesting for statewide offices after 1920.

In the 1940s, a "Lily White," B. Carroll Reece, first district congressman, became the Republican power broker in Tennessee. He also became a power in the national hierarchy, once serving as chairman of the Republican National Committee. Because he had no desire to share power, the last thing Reece wanted was for a Republican to be elected governor or to either of the United States Senate posts. According to lore, Reece maintained his hegemony by cooperating with Democrats during the heyday of Crump and McKellar. The Republicans voted in Democratic primaries for Crump-endorsed candidates and then placed only token candidates in races for governor and senator. In return, Reece and other Republican leaders were rewarded with federal and state patronage and other services and a pledge to avoid meddling in Republican affairs. It is impossible to verify the alleged cooperation. No doubt there was some trading but the amount was probably exaggerated by contemporaries. There is abundant evidence, however, that many Republicans often voted in Democratic primaries and, in close races, may well have been the determining factor in the outcomes. Whatever the case, Reece preferred the status quo. An aggressive Republican effort to win a statewide election could have broken the *modus vivendi*. But in the postwar years, the old Republican leaders in East Tennessee began to die off, thus bringing an end to the safe baronies. At the same time, the Grand Old Party began to breathe new life.

The Republican revival began soon after the war. White middle- and upper-class Democrats grew increasingly unhappy with the liberal economic policies of the national Democratic party. Republican presidential candidates were thus more attractive than those offered by the Democrats. Dwight David Eisenhower carried Tennessee in 1952 and 1956 and Richard Milhous Nixon defeated John Fitzgerald Kennedy in the presidential race in Tennessee in 1960. Yet, during those same years, the New Deal coalition kept Senators Gore and Kefauver and Governor Clement in office. By the mid-1960s, as a result of changing social and economic conditions wrought by industrialization, urbanization, and especially the civil rights movement, the Grand Old Party seemed to gain strength in numbers. The increases were achieved where the black population was large. In Memphis and Shelby County, the urban center with the greatest concentration of blacks, the white suburban fringe began voting Republican in significant numbers. But while many Tennessee Democrats were converting to Republicanism, blacks, because of the national party's commitment to civil rights, became more solidly Democratic. Their vote became crucial in statewide elections. Ironically, the Democratic General Assembly, under court order to reapportion itself, acknowledged changed voting patterns in Shelby County. District lines were drawn to protect a Democratic seat but it allowed a black to be elected to the legislature in 1964. Thus, by the mid-1960s, the New Deal Coalition collapsed and the Republican party began to challenge the Democrats with a vigor unknown since Reconstruction.

In 1964, the Grand Old Party made its most serious bid for statewide offices in almost half a century. Both United States Senate posts were before the electorate: a full term for the seat occupied by Albert Gore and the unexpired term of the late Estes Kefauver. When Kefauver died in 1963, Governor Clement appointed as interim caretaker a longtime politician and ally from Morristown, Herbert Sanford Walters. Clement then announced as a candidate for the Democratic nomination to fill the remaining two years of the term. His opponents were Ross Bass, sixth district congressman who had earned a reputation in Congress as a liberal, and M. M. Bullard, a Newport businessman and friend to the late Senator Kefauver. For the first time in his career, Clement lost a race. Bass, with an absolute majority, polled a hundred thousand more votes than the governor and Bullard was a poor third. Gore had only token opposition in the primary. The Republicans placed two strong contenders in both Senate races. Opposing Bass was the attractive, clean-cut, and articulate Howard Baker, Jr., son of former congressman Howard Baker, Sr. Gore's opponent was a Memphis business executive, Dan Heflin Kuykendall. Both races were close and polled more than a million votes. Gore won reelection by only 87,000 votes and Bass won by 81,000. Although defeated, Republicans were gratified by the showing of both candidates. The outcome of the general election foretold more enthusiastic activity two years later.

Despite the good showing in the senatorial contests, the Democratic presidential candidate carried Tennessee for the first time since 1948. Lyndon Baines Johnson, who assumed the presidency upon the assassination of President Kennedy in 1963, was challenged by Senator Barry Goldwater, the Republican nominee. Goldwater damaged his chances by suggesting that the Tennessee Valley Authority, then a sacrosanct agency in the Volunteer State, be sold to private enterprise. No doubt some Tennesseans voted for Johnson because he was a fellow Southerner. Johnson's victory in the state was not an overwhelming one and black votes were a crucial factor.

In 1966, the electorate was confronted with races for a full Senate term and a gubernatorial contest. The Senate race was a duplicate of the short-term race in 1964. After attempting to mend his fences in the intervening two years, Clement entered the campaign against Senator Bass for the Democratic nomination. After considering running against Gore for the Senate in 1964, Buford Ellington decided to try for the governorship once again. His opponent was John Jay Hooker, Jr., the son of a Nashville attorney and a long-time political activist. In contrast to the conservative Ellington, Hooker was a liberal in the mold of John F. Kennedy. The Clement and Ellington campaigns were kept separate. The coalition had been weakened by the passing of some of the older leaders as well as defections. Yet Clement retained enough of his loyalists to carry on a spirited race and he narrowly defeated Bass for the nomination. There is evidence that crossover Republican votes were crucial to Clement's mere 18,000-vote margin out of 750,000 cast. Ellington, perhaps because of his conservative image, had an easier time, defeating Hooker by 414,000 to 360,000. Howard Baker, Jr. was once again the Republican nominee for the Senate. Perhaps the electorate had grown weary of Clement and the Republicans had an attractive candidate in Baker. Clement went down to a stinging defeat by 100,000 votes, and Tennessee, for the first time since Reconstruction, sent a Republican to the United States Senate. Interestingly, the Grand Old Party did not offer a candidate for the governorship and Ellington returned to the governor's office virtually unopposed. Still, the Republicans made a significant gain when Memphian Dan Kuykendall won the ninth district congressional race, defeating the Democratic nominee, James O. Patterson, Jr., the first black to win a major nomination.

The presidential race in 1968 was indicative of the momentum of Republicans in Tennessee and declining fortunes for the Democrats. The Republican nominee, Richard Nixon, won the state. The Democratic candidate, liberal Hubert Horatio Humphrey, came in a poor third behind the second-place George Wallace who ran as an independent in protest to liberal economic and racial policies of the national government. Moreover, in part as a result of reapportionment, Republicans won narrow control of the lower house of the General Assembly for the biannuam 1969-1970. Then in 1970, the Grand Old Party swept the statewide offices.

The election of 1970, which would determine a governor and a senator, was crucial. Ellington was unable to succeed himself so the Democratic gubernatorial primary attracted a large number of hopefuls. Only two, John J. Hooker and State Senator Stanley Snodgrass, who had the backing of the Ellington administration, emerged as legitimate contenders. There were five candidates for the Republican nomination, but only three, Winfield Dunn, a personable Memphis dentist who had once been a Democrat, Maxey Jarman, a Nashville businessman, and William Jenkins, a Knoxville attorney, attracted attention. The struggle between Hooker and Snodgrass was a bruising one, but the former defeated the state senator by almost 70,000 votes in a low turnout. With four other candidates in the race, however, the victor became the nominee by a plurality of approximately forty-four percent of the vote. In the Republican primary, Dunn led the balloting by 11,000 over the nearest rival and won with a plurality of only thirty-four percent of the total votes cast.

In the race for the Democratic senatorial nomination, the incumbent, Gore, faced four rivals but it developed that only one, Hudley Crockett, a Nashville television newsman, proved to be a serious contender. Senator Gore's support in the state had declined sharply largely because of his liberal image, his opposition to the war in Vietnam, and the fact that he had not kept his fences mended in Tennessee. Crockett came close and Gore won by only 31,000 out of just below 529,000 votes cast. In the Republican primary, third district congressman, William Emerson Brock, III, the scion of a wealthy candy manufacturer, won the nomination easily. In the general election campaign, some Democratic leaders, including

Governor Ellington, unhappy with the liberal nominees, "took a walk," and withheld endorsement. The ideological rift in the Democracy may have been the decisive factor for both races were relatively close. Brock defeated the veteran Gore by 42,000 votes. Dunn won by a larger margin, 66,000 votes out of over a million cast. Both Republicans carried the traditional party stronghold in East Tennessee by a sizable vote as well as Shelby County. They also did well in suburban areas of the state.

For the first time since Reconstruction, the Republican party controlled all three major statewide offices. In 1972, further gains were made. As a result of the 1970 census, Tennessee lost a congressional seat. Despite Democratic gerrymandering attempts, another Republican won another congressional seat, giving the party control of five of the eight posts. Senator Baker won reelection easily and Republican candidate Richard Nixon carried Tennessee by a landslide. The Republican successes after 1964 led contemporary observers to the conclusion that the Volunteer State had arrived as a two-party state. A chapter on Tennessee in a volume on politics in the contemporary South was entitled "Tennessee: Genuine Two Party State." Scholars Lee Greene and Jack Holmes, writing in 1972, concluded that "Tennessee ought now to be dropped (if it ever belonged there) from the list of one-party-states." These observations may have been a bit premature. The pendulum slowly began to shift back to the Democrats after 1972.

The Republican majority in the lower house of the General Assembly was of short duration. After the election of 1970, the Democrats regained a majority and within four years, both houses were safely controlled by the Democracy. In 1974, the Democrats regained the governorship. There were no less than seven contenders in the Democratic primary and included Hudley Crockett, Stanley Snodgrass, Knoxville banker Jake Butcher, and Chattanooga businessman Franklin Haney. The victor, with only twenty-five percent of the vote and 16,000 more than his nearest rival, was former sixth district congressman, Leonard Ray Blanton. A contractor from McNairy County, Blanton had won the Democratic senatorial nomination in 1972 but was defeated by Howard Baker by 275,000 votes. The winner in the far less crowded Republican primary was a relatively youthful unknown, Lamar Alexander from

Maryville. Alexander had served briefly in the Nixon White House, managed Governor Dunn's campaign in 1970, and was allied with Senator Baker. Blanton defeated Alexander by well over one hundred thousand votes. The loser carried East Tennessee and parts of West Tennessee, including Shelby County, but Blanton's lead in traditional Democratic areas was too great. In addition, a Democrat and the first woman to be elected to Congress, Marilyn Lloyd (Bouquard), defeated the Republican third district congressman, LaMar Baker. Moreover, the Volunteer State sent its first black to Congress. A black Democrat from Memphis, Harold Ford, defeated incumbent Dan Kuykendall by a razor-thin margin for the eighth district seat. Democrats now controlled the congressional delegation five to three.

Two years later the Democracy made a serious bid for the Senate seat occupied by William E. Brock, whose term had been singularly lackluster. The two leading hopefuls for the Democratic nomination were John J. Hooker and James Sasser. The latter had once served as youth director for Senator Kefauver, and for three years prior to the Senate race he was chairman of the state Democratic Committee. Sasser defeated Hooker soundly and then swamped Brock in the general election. Thus a Senate seat returned to the Democrats. Moreover, a Democratic presidential candidate carried the Volunteer State for only the second time since 1948. James Earl "Jimmy" Carter polled fifty-six percent of the vote to only forty-three percent for the Republican candidate, Gerald Ford. Many Tennesseans probably voted for Carter because he was a native of Georgia and a fellow Southerner. The black vote was also important to Carter's victory in Tennessee. The Democratic momentum, however, slowed two years later.

A constitutional amendment ratified in 1975 allowed a governor to succeed himself but Governor Blanton declined to run. The Democratic primary then became a free-for-all with eight candidates. Only three, Jake Butcher, Robert Clement, son of the late governor, and Nashville mayor Richard Fulton, were serious contenders. Outspending the rest, Butcher won a plurality with forty-one percent of the vote. After four years spent in improving his image and building an organization, Lamar Alexander garnered the Republican nod with virtually no opposition. The Democrats faced a difficult gubernatorial race. For one thing, scandals in the Blanton administration had led to convictions of members of his official family for payoffs. The administration was also alleged to be selling pardons. Many were displeased with Butcher's spending in the primary and some of Clement's loyalists were bitter and refused to endorse the nominee. The clean-cut, personable Alexander defeated the Democrat by a sizable majority and fifty-six percent of the vote. The Grand Old Party had reclaimed the governor's office. Blanton left the governorship under a cloud. In order to forestall further pardons, the General Assembly set an early and hasty swearing in of Alexander. Blanton was later convicted in a federal court for selling liquor licenses. In the senatorial race, Howard Baker received the Republican nod over token opposition and Public Service commissioner Jane Eskind, and won by a plurality in a three-way race in the Democratic primary. Baker disposed of Eskind by a margin of three to two. In 1980, the Republican presidential candidate, Ronald Reagan, defeated President Carter in Tennessee but by less than 5,000 votes. Reagan carried the traditional Republican strongholds plus Shelby County.

Both statewide primaries in 1982 were unexciting. Governor Alexander won renomination virtually unopposed. In the Democratic gubernatorial race, Knoxville mayor Randy Tyree won by a comfortable margin over State Senator Anna Belle Clement O'Brien, sister of the late governor Clement. Democratic Senator Sasser was renominated and sixth district congressman Robin Beard, an archconservative, was given the Republican nod. There was widespread evidence of ticket splitting in the general election. The governor was reelected by a margin of 238,000 votes and close to sixty percent of the total. Senator Sasser won reelection by an even wider margin, 298,000 and sixty-two percent of the vote. Congressional reapportionment after the 1980 census awarded Tennessee another district and a Democrat was elected to the seat. Once again in 1984, a Republican presidential candidate carried the Volunteer State. Reagan won by a landslide and fifty-nine percent of the total vote. In contrast, the Democrats captured a United State Senate seat. In 1984, Senator Howard Baker announced that he would retire at the end of his term. Unfortunately, the Republicans did not have an attractive available leader except Governor Alexander. The governor, however, rejected overtures that he enter the race, declaring that he was committed to completing his term. The nomination then went almost by default to the uninspiring State Senator Victor Ashe of Knoxville. It was almost inevitable that fourth district congressman Albert Gore, Jr., son of the former senator, would seek the Democratic nomination. In four terms in the House of Representatives, Gore had been hardworking and aggressive. His political availability was so attractive that he discouraged others from making a bid and he received the Democratic nomination without contest. Gore went on to defeat his Republican opponent by sixty-one percent of the vote and by an even wider margin than Reagan's landslide. Thus, after eighteen years, both of Tennessee's United States Senate seats were occupied by Democrats, but the governorship remained in the hands of the Grand Old Party.

It seems evident that between 1965 and 1985, the Republican party emerged as a strong rival to the Democrats. Republicans won four of five presidential races, three of five gubernatorial contests, and three of six senatorial terms, at one point controlled a majority of congressional seats, and briefly captured control of the lower house in the General Assembly. Even the more casual observer would agree with Greene and Holmes that the Grand Old Party was no longer "just visiting" in the Volunteer State.

There was a correlation between the resurgence of the Republican party and the trends of industrialization and urbanization, reapportionment, and the civil rights movement. The causal relationship was complex and therefore difficult to measure. It is possible, however, to suggest some reasons linking causation with correlation. It seems likely that new industrial managers, many of whom were migrants from beyond the South, were already Republicans or held economic views compatible with Republicanism. The rising white-collar middle and upper classes who populated the suburban fringes found the economic conservatism of Republicanism attractive. Moreover, the social conservatism of the Grand Old Party was congenial with the beliefs of many blue-collar workers. More than anything else, the civil rights movement chipped away at the New Deal coalition and the civil rights acts passed by Congress and subsequent equal opportunity measures supplied the coup de grace. The Second Reconstruction converted many white Democrats into Republicans and the Grand Old Party's greatest gains in numbers were in areas of the heaviest black population.

The Republican party stood to benefit by reapportionment, but the gains were not large. There was some increased representation from Republican East Tennessee. The constitutional convention of 1965, conforming to the demands of the "one man one vote" mandate of the Supreme Court, provided for representation by population in both houses of the General Assembly. Moreover, at-large districts were abolished and single-member districts established. At-large districts had long been used in urban centers as a device to reduce or mitigate the power of large minority voting blocks or in some cases, suburbs. The switch to single-member districts virtually assured an increase in black representation. It also meant that the suburban fringes of cities, where voters seemed to be more philosophically sympathetic to the countryside and were voting Republican in increased numbers, would gain in representation in the legislature. A concession was made to Republicans in congressional redistricting. A congressional district was created that included Whitehaven and suburban South Memphis, Republican hill counties in West Tennessee and across Middle Tennessee to the fringe of West Nashville. This district was certain to elect a Republican but a Democratic district was preserved. The central city of Memphis, which has a heavy black population, was established as a congressional district. A black would be elected but he would be a Democrat. Otherwise, judicious gerrymandering limited Republicans' gains in the legislature. Ironically, the older central cities which had expected benefits from reapportionment, gained little at the time when they were beginning to experience problems that plagued cities all across the nation: a decaying core, capital flight, revenue flight, and "white flight" to suburbia.

Like the Republicans, Tennessee's black minority received short shrift from reapportionment and for that matter, the Second Reconstruction. On the surface, it appears that federal edicts to end school segregation and discrimination in the economy have succeeded. By the 1980s, schools in Tennessee were integrated and it is common to see blacks in jobs denied to them a few years earlier. Despite the apparent improvements in the economic conditions of

blacks, the gap between the races in the Volunteer State is as wide
if not wider than before the civil rights movement began. To be sure,
many have achieved middle-class status, but blacks in general remain at the bottom of the socioeconomic scale, live in substandard
housing, and suffer from high unemployment. Moreover, segregation persists; *de facto* segregation has replaced *de jure* segregation. Blacks are trapped in urban ghettos or limited by economic
reasons to living in central cities or other areas abandoned by whites.
Blacks serve on city councils and are in other administrative positions and urban black enclaves send representatives to the state legislature. There are consistently about three in the State Senate and
about eight in the lower house, but these numbers fall far short of
the percentage of the black population in the state. The gerrymandering of black districts was a concession to the Second Reconstruction; an innovation was reconciled with tradition. The black vote
was isolated and minimized and the small number in the legislative
body exercise little influence. As a number of scholars have noted,
recent elections make it clear that race remains a politically vital issue. The gap between the races in Tennessee remains wide and the
racial issue polarized.

The period from 1965 to 1985 was a time of political change and
party realignment. Yet a close examination of the trends after 1965
reveals that the Republican resurgence has been more apparent
than real. The Grand Old Party did indeed pick up strength in new
areas of Tennessee and is much better organized statewide, but the
Democracy is still the dominant party by almost two to one. Polls
consistently reveal that forty to forty-five percent of Tennesseans
are Democrats while only twenty to twenty-five percent are Republicans. The most significant change has been the increase in the
number of independent or nonaligned voters, a pattern that is na-
tionwide and not exclusive to the Volunteer State. Party labels are
not as important as in the past and split-ticket voting is common.
Present-day campaigning requires projecting a positive image,
particularly through the medium of television. Viewers tend to form
strong perceptions as to which candidate is more decisive and capable or stronger and more likable. The electorate casts ballots for
those who succeed in projecting more style than substance, regardless of the party. Still, the Democratic majority is clearly indicated

in the makeup of the General Assembly. Except for one brief interlude, the Democrats have consistently held comfortable majorities in the legislature. The chief problem of the Democracy in Tennessee is a traditional one. The party has long been troubled by factional disputes. The party also contains conservatives, liberals, blacks, organized labor, intellectuals, and other groups that are easily divided over substantive, philosophical, and emotional issues. The profound and rapid changes since World War II have produced a profusion of divisive problems for Democrats. It has largely been cleavages within the Democratic party rather than the growing strength of the Grand Old Party that resulted in the latter winning statewide elections after 1965. Since Reconstruction it has been axiomatic that Republicans can win state offices only when Democrats are divided. Although it is possible for an especially attractive Republican to win with independent votes, the axiom remains essentially true in the 1980s.

Epilogue

In the half century since Franklin D. Roosevelt described the South, which included Tennessee, as "the nation's number one economic problem," the physical landscape of the Volunteer State has been dramatically altered. Millions of acres of eroded, worn-out lands have been reclaimed and reforestation has created vast stands of timber. Tenant shacks have all but disappeared and farms generally give the appearance of prosperity. Large man-made lakes not only add beauty to the state but provide recreation for both Tennesseans and tourists. The state is predominantly industrial and urban and most people are employed in industrial, mercantile, and service establishments. More than sixty percent of the people in Tennessee live in cities. Although the metropolitan areas suffer problems similar to those in the rest of the country—central city blight and suburban sprawl—the state's urban centers seem to be thriving. There are skyscrapers, high-rise hotels with revolving restaurants on top, and convention centers. Airports are centers of busy activity and the cities are laced together with expressways that speed the flow of traffic. A large middle class lives in comfortable, well-built houses in suburbia convenient to well-stocked shopping centers. The new middle class can also be found in small towns and the countryside. Almost every small town has shopping centers with discount department stores and fast-food restaurants. Tennessee in the 1980s gives evidence of prosperity, but the veneer of prosperity is deceiving.

If it was the expectation of the proponents of economic growth that industrialization would place Tennessee's economy on a par with states outside the South, the goal failed to materialize. The average income in the Volunteer State remains well below the national average. Moreover, the incidence of poverty remains above the national average. Widespread, grinding poverty among both black and white and rural and urban dwellers still exists. Tennessee also ranks near the bottom in the quality of public service and its institutions. With a tax base that is inadequate and regressive, Tennessee is unable to fund such services as education, highways, transportation, and welfare at levels comparable to states beyond the South. In the 1970s, commentators began predicting that the South was on the verge of growth of such magnitude that the region would soon become an economic paradise. It was not long before the "Sunbelt South" media hype seemed like a cruel hoax. Moreover, instead of a boom, Tennessee experienced a recession. The decline of heavy industries in the so-called "Frostbelt North" was partially reflected in Tennessee in the closing of some industries and loss of jobs in the state. In addition, there was an exodus of some small industries overseas in search of cheaper labor. In certain areas of the state, the unemployment rate far exceeds the national rate. In the mid-1980s, the South and Tennessee, remain "the nation's number one economic problem."

The reasons why Tennessee's goal of economic parity failed to materialize are many and complex. For one thing, the state began and long existed in a colonial condition, depending on outside investors and absentee owners who drained off capital and profits. More significant, perhaps, was the difficulty of reconciling beliefs, values, and norms with an urban-industrial culture. Tennesseans wanted the economic stimulus of industrialization but not some of the side effects. Because the presence of strong labor unions tends to result in higher prevailing wage rates, established business interests were hostile to organized labor. Moreover, unions seemed foreign to rural values. Thus industry was recruited because of the lower labor costs of a nonunion labor force and the promise of tax breaks. To be sure, some union industries settled in Tennessee and there was some increase in membership, but organized labor was never a large vested interest and therefore exercised little political power. In fact, politicians could ordinarily ignore labor unions on most issues. Too, the rank and file sometimes voted contrary to the dictates of their leadership. If organized labor had been unified and strong, wages in Tennessee would likely have been higher and more in line with wages in the rest of the nation.

Anti-union sentiment encouraged the establishment of labor-intensive, low-wage paying manufacturing in Tennessee. Such industries as textile, garment, and shoe factories were located in small towns and even in the country. County and small-town elite, businessmen, bankers, and large land owners welcomed modest non-union manufacturing for it constituted no threat to the social order. Small industries had several advantages. They absorbed surplus agricultural labor, local merchants profited from the payrolls spent in the communities, and the low wages did not compete with prevailing wage rates. The last thing the social and political hierarchy wanted was unionized industries that might threaten local wage levels. By maintaining control of the labor force and wage rates, the hierarchy, as James C. Cobb suggests, created a new labor-intensive, low-wage system that was not unlike the old traditional plantation agricultural system. At any rate, cultural patterns, the folkways and mores of Tennessee, were relatively unchanged by industrialization and indeed, the new economic system served as a buttress for maintaining a caste system and the status quo. The dominant social class remained unchallenged.

The dominant social and political hierarchy in Tennessee in the 1980s, regardless of political labels, holds essentially conservative, rural values not unlike those of a century ago. They hold steadfastly to the belief that the government that governs best, governs least. Moreover, the government should be fiscally sound and if taxes are necessary, such levies as the regressive sales tax are preferable to progressive taxation. They are committed to *laissez-faire* and nonregulation except in cases where subsidies and regulation benefit the hierarchy. They do approve of education, especially vocational training and expenditures for highways to benefit the economy. Beyond that, proposals to improve the general welfare or reform the tax structure meet stiff resistance. Tennessee's social and political leadership of the 1980s subscribe to an ideological persuasion that differs very little from the Bourbonism of the post-Civil War era.

In noting cultural continuity, historian George Brown Tindall has, on more than one occasion, quoted an old French proverb: "the

more it changes, the more it is the same thing." The hypothesis of
this volume posits that despite great changes in both the physical
and cultural landscape in Tennessee since the Civil War, conservative Bourbon beliefs, values, and norms have persisted relatively
unaltered; that a community of interests, when faced with change
or demands for reform, adjusted, accommodated to reform, and
reconciled innovation with tradition. During redemption, when
threatened by a Whig takeover, Bourbons accepted just enough
Whiggery to beat back the threat. Again, the Bourbons defeated the
agrarian revolters by accepting the less noxious demands of the
Populists. After the turn of the century, the Bourbons joined the
progressives as the business progressives. Perhaps the greatest
threat to Bourbonism came from the New Deal coalition, but the
dominant community of interests was able to reach accommoda-
tion with New Deal reforms to retain hegemony. Finally, post-World
War II Bourbonism was able to adjust to the demands of the bull-
dozer revolution and the Second Reconstruction to remain in the
ascendancy. The conservative values and beliefs—antistatism, *laissez-faire*, antiunionism, and white supremacy—remain dominant.
The names, faces, and issues in the political arena in Tennessee have
changed over the years, but an underlying set of conservative cultural patterns have persisted. The more it changes, the more it is
the same thing.

Appendix

TABLE 1

Governors of Tennessee since 1860			
(D) Democrat		(R) Republican	
Isham G. Harris (D)	1861-1862	Tom C. Rye (D)	1915-1917
Andrew Johnson[1] (D)	1862-1865		1917-1919
William G. Brownlow (R)	1865-1867	Albert H. Roberts (D)	1919-1921
	1867-1869	Alfred A. Taylor (R)	1921-1923
DeWitt C.Senter (R)	1869[2]	Austin Peay (D)	1923-1925
	1869-1871		1925-1927
John C. Brown (D)	1871-1873		1927[4]
	1873-1875	Henry H. Horton (D)	1927-1929
James D. Porter (D)	1875-1877		1929-1931
	1877-1879		1931-1933
Albert S. Marks (D)	1879-1881	Hill McAlister (D)	1933-1935
Alvin Hawkins (R)	1881-1883		1935-1937
William B. Bate (D)	1883-1885	Gordon Browning (D)	1937-1939
	1885-1887	Prentice Cooper (D)	1939-1941
Robert L. Taylor (D)	1887-1889		1941-1943
	1889-1891		1943-1945
John P. Buchanan (D)	1891-1893	Jim Nance McCord (D)	1945-1947
Peter Turney (D)	1893-1895		1947-1949
	1895-1897	Gordon Browning (D)	1949-1951
Robert L. Taylor (D)	1897-1899		1951-1953
Benton McMillin (D)	1899-1901	Frank G. Clement (D)	1953-1955
	1901-1903		1955-1959
James B. Frazier (D)	1903-1905	Buford Ellington (D)	1959-1963
	1905[3]	Frank G. Clement (D)	1963-1967
John I. Cox (D)	1905-1907	Buford Ellington (D)	1967-1971
Malcolm R. Patterson (D)	1907-1909	Winfield Dunn (R)	1971-1975
	1909-1911	Ray Blanton (D)	1975-1979
Ben W. Hooper (R)	1911-1913	Lamar Alexander (R)	1979-1983
	1913-1915		1983-

[1]Appointed military governor by President Lincoln.
[2]Became governor upon Brownlow's resignation in February.
[3]Frazier resigned to accept election to the Senate two months into his second term.
[4]Peay died in October, nine months into his third term.

TABLE 2

United States Senators since 1860			
(D) Democrat (R) Republican			
* Interim appointment † Elected to unexpired term			
A. P. O. Nicholson (D)	1859-1861[1]	Andrew Johnson (D)	1857-1862[2]
Joseph S. Fowler (R)	1866-1871[3]	James D. Patterson (R)	1866-1869[4]
		William G. Brownlow (R)	1869-1875
Henry D. Cooper (D)	1871-1877	Andrew Johnson (D)	1875[5]
		David M. Key* (D)	1875-1877
Isham G. Harris (D)	1877-1883	James E. Bailey† (D)	1877-1881
Isham G. Harris (D)	1883-1889	Howell E. Jackson (D)	1881-1887
Isham G. Harris (D)	1889-1895	William B. Bate (D)	1887-1893
Isham G. Harris (D)	1895-1897[6]	William B. Bate (D)	1893-1899
Thomas B. Turley* (D)	1897-1898		
Thomas B. Turley† (D)	1898-1901	William B. Bate (D)	1899-1905
Edward W. Carmack (D)	1901-1907	William B. Bate (D)	1905[7]
Robert L. Taylor (D)[8]	1907-1912	James B. Frazier† (D)	1905-1911
Newell Sanders* (D)	1912-1913	Luke Lea (D)	1911-1917
William R. Webb†	1913		
John K. Shields (D)	1913-1919	Kenneth D. McKellar (D)	1917-1923
John K. Shields (D)	1919-1925	Kenneth D. McKellar (D)	1923-1929
Lawrence D. Tyson (D)	1925-1929[9]		
William E. Brock* (D)	1929-1931	Kenneth D. McKellar (D)	1929-1935
William E. Brock† (D)	1931		
Cordell Hull (D)	1931-1933[10]		
Nathan Bachman* (D)	1933-1935		
Nathan Bachman† (D)	1935-1937	Kenneth D. McKellar (D)	1935-1941
Nathan Bachman (D)	1937[11]		
George L. Berry* (D)	1937-1938		
Tom Stewart† (D)	1938-1943	Kenneth D. McKellar (D)	1941-1947
Tom Stewart (D)	1943-1949	Kenneth D. McKellar (D)	1947-1953
Estes Kefauver (D)	1949-1955	Albert Gore, Sr. (D)	1953-1959
Estes Kefauver (D)	1955-1961		
Estes Kefauver (D)	1961-1963[12]	Albert Gore, Sr. (D)	1959-1965
Hubert S. Walters* (D)	1963-1965		
Ross Bass† (D)	1965-1967	Albert Gore, Sr. (D)	1965-1971
Howard Baker, Jr. (R)	1967-1973		
Howard Baker, Jr. (R)	1973-1979	William E. Brock III (R)	1971-1977
Howard Baker, Jr. (R)	1979-1985	James Sasser (D)	1977-1983
Albert Gore, Jr. (D)	1985-	James Sasser (D)	1983-

[1]Resigned when Tennessee seceded in 1861.
[2]Retained seat when Tennessee seceded in 1861.
[3]Elected to the long term when Tennessee was readmitted to the Union in 1866.
[4]Elected to the short term when Tennessee was readmitted to the Union in 1866.
[5]Died in July 1875.   [6]Died in July 1897.
[7]Died in March 1905 only a week into his new term.   [8]Died in March 1912.
[9]Died in August 1929.   [10]Resigned in 1933 to become secretary of state.
[11]Died in April 1937.   [12]Died in August 1963.

TABLE 3

Vote in Gubernatorial Elections, 1861–1916

| Parties: (D) Democrat (C) Conservative (G) Greenback (I) Independent |
| (P) Populist (Pr) Prohibition (R) Republican (U) Union |

• 1861 •	**• 1890 •**
Isham G. Harris (D).........74,973	Lewis T. Baxter (R).........76,081
William A. Polk (U).........43,313	John P. Buchanan (D).........114,240
• 1865 •	D. C. Kelly (Pr).........11,003
William G. Brownlow (R).........23,222[1]	**• 1892 •**
• 1867 •	John P. Buchanan (P).........31,520
William G. Brownlow (R).........74,484	Peter Turney (D).........126,250
Emerson Etheridge (C).........22,438	George Winstead (R).........100,023
• 1869 •	**• 1894[4] •**
D. W. C. Senter (R).........120,333	H. Clay Evans (R).........92,266
William B. Stokes (C).........55,036	A. L. Mims (P).........23,088
• 1870 •	Peter Turney (D).........94,620
John C. Brown (D).........78,979	**• 1896 •**
William Wisener (R).........41,500	A. L. Mims (P).........11,966
• 1872 •	Robert L. Taylor (D).........156,333
John C. Brown (D).........97,700	George N. Tillman (R).........149,374
Alfred A. Freeman (R).........89,089	**• 1898 •**
• 1874 •	James A. Fowler (R).........72,640
James D. Porter (D).........105,061	Benton McMillin (D).........105,640
Horace Maynard (R).........55,847	**• 1900 •**
• 1876 •	John R. McCall (R).........110,835
James D. Porter (D).........123,740	Benton McMillin (D).........145,708
Dorsey B. Thomas (R).........73,697	**• 1902 •**
• 1878 •	H. T. Campbell (R).........59,007
R. M. Edwards (G).........15,155	James B. Frazier (D).........98,902
Albert S. Marks (D).........89,958	**• 1904 •**
E. M. Wright (R).........42,284	James B. Frazier (D).........131,503
• 1880 •	J. M. Littleton (R).........103,409
Alvin Hawkins (R).........103,964	**• 1906 •**
S. F. Wilson (D)[2].........57,080	H. Clay Evans (R).........92,804
John V. Wright (D)[3].........78,783	M. R. Patterson (D).........111,856
• 1882 •	**• 1908 •**
William B. Bate (D).........120,637	M. R. Patterson (D).........133,166
Alvin Hawkins (R).........93,168	G. N. Tillman (R).........113,233
• 1884 •	**• 1910 •**
William B. Bate (D).........132,201	Ben W. Hooper (R).........133,075
Frank T. Reid (R).........125,246	Robert L. Taylor (D).........121,694
• 1886 •	**• 1912 •**
Alfred A. Taylor (R).........109,837	Ben W. Hooper (R).........124,641
Robert L. Taylor (D).........126,628	Benton McMillin (D).........116,610
• 1888 •	**• 1914 •**
Samuel W. Hawkins (R).........139,014	Ben W. Hooper (R).........116,667
Robert L. Taylor (D).........155,888	Tom C. Rye (D).........137,656
	• 1916 •
	John W. Overall (R).........117,819
	Tom C. Rye (D).........146,759

[1]Five other candidates polled a total of only 35 votes.
[2]Low-tax Democrat. [3]State-credit Democrat.
[4]The initial count gave Evans 105,104 to Turney's 104,356, but the General Assembly invalidated many votes, subtracting more than 12,000 from Evans's total and less than 10,000 from Turney's total.

TABLE 4

Vote in Gubernatorial Elections since the Institution of Party Primaries in 1918

DEMOCRATIC PARTY			REPUBLICAN PARTY		
CANDIDATE	PRIMARY	GENERAL ELECTION	CANDIDATE	PRIMARY	GENERAL ELECTION
• 1918 •					
A. H. Roberts	64,191	98,626	H. B. Lindsey		59,519
Austin Peay	51,971				
• 1920 •					
A. H. Roberts	67,886	185,890	Alf Taylor	12,385	229,143
W. R. Crabtree	44,853		J. M. Littleton	2,176	
• 1922 •					
Austin Peay	63,940	141,002	Alf Taylor		102,586
Benton McMillin	59,992				
Harry Hannah	24,062				
• 1924 •					
Austin Peay	125,031	152,002	T. F. Peck		121,328
John R. Neal	33,199				
• 1926 •					
Austin Peay	96,545	84,979	Walter White	6,295	46,238
Hill McAlister	88,448				
• 1928 •					
Henry Horton	97,333	195,545	Raleigh Hopkins		124,733
Hill McAlister	92,015				
Lewis Pope	27,720				
• 1930 •					
Henry Horton	145,991	153,341	G. Arthur Bruce	60,447	85,558
L. E. Gwinn	101,285		Harry T. Burns	32,815	
• 1932 •					
Hill McAlister	116,832	168,075	John E. McCall	61,113	120,497
Lewis Pope	107,449		Hal Clements	50,159	
M. R. Patterson	59,392				
Lewis Pope, Independent, polled 107,026 in the general election.					
• 1934 •					
Hill McAlister	191,450	198,743	John E. McCall	56,133	
Lewis Pope	137,253		Will H. Clark	33,712	
Lewis Pope, Independent, polled 122,965 in the general election. The Republican candidate withdrew and endorsed Pope.					
• 1936 •					
Gordon Browning	243,463	332,523	Dwayne Maddox	35,928	
Burgin Dossett	109,170		Henry Camp, Jr.	23,469	
			P. H. Thatch		78,292
Thatch replaced Maddox as the Republican nominee.					

continued

continued   **TABLE 4**

• 1938 •					
Prentice Cooper	231,852	210,568	Howard H. Baker		83,031
Gordon Browning	158,854				

• 1940 •					
Prentice Cooper	237,319	323,466	G. Arthur Bruce		125,254
George Dempster	44,122				

• 1942 •					
Prentice Cooper	171,259	120,146	C. N. Frazier		51,120
J. Ridley Mitchell	124,037				

• 1944 •					
Jim Nance McCord	132,466	275,746	John W. Kilgo	35,463	158,742
			W. D. Lowe	13,425	

• 1946 •					
Jim Nance McCord	187,119	149,937	W. D. Lowe	33,269	73,222
Gordon Browning	120,535				

• 1948 •					
Gordon Browning	267,855	363,903	Roy Acuff	90,140	179,957
Jim Nance McCord	183,948		R. M. Murray	21,765	

• 1950 •					
Gordon Browning	267,855	184,437			
Clifford Allen	208,634				

John R. Neal, Independent, received 51,757 ballots in the general election.

• 1952 •					
Frank G. Clement	302,491	640,290	R. Beecher Witt	40,263	166,377
Gordon Browning	245,166				
Clifford Allen	75,269				
Clifford Pierce	24,191				

• 1954 •					
Frank G. Clement	481,808	281,291			
Gordon Browning	195,156				

John R. Neal, Independent, received 39,574 ballots in the general election.

• 1958 •					
Buford Ellington	213,415	248,874	R. L. Peters, Jr.	18,323	
A. T. Taylor	204,629		Hansell Profitt	12,565	
Edmund Orgill	204,382		Thomas P. Wall		35,938
Clifford Allen	56,854				

Thomas P. Wall replaced Peters as the Republican nominee.
Jim Nance McCord, Independent, received 136,399 ballots in the general election.

• 1962 •					
Frank G. Clement	309,333	315,648	Hubert D. Patty	51,969	99,884
P. R. Olgiata	211,812				
William W. Farris	202,813				

William R. Anderson, Independent, received 203,765 ballots in the general election.

continued

continued   **TABLE 4**

• 1966 •					
Buford Ellington	413,950	532,998			
John J. Hooker, Jr.	360,105				
Two independents received a total of 114,823 ballots in the general election.					
• 1970 •					
John J. Hooker, Jr.	261,580	509,521	Winfield Dunn	81,475	575,777
Stanley Snodgrass	193,199		Maxey Jarman	70,420	
Robert L. Taylor	90,009		William Jenkins	50,910	
Douglas Heinsohn, American Party, received 22,945 ballots in the general election.					
• 1974 •					
Ray Blanton	148,062	576,833	Lamar Alexander	120,773	455,467
Jake Butcher	132,173		Nat Winston	90,980	
Tom Wiseman	89,061		Dortch Oldham	35,683	
Hudley Crockett	86,852				
Franklin Haney	84,155				
Stanley Snodgrass	40,211				
• 1978 •					
Jake Butcher	320,329	523,495	Lamar Alexander	230,922	661,959
Bob Clement	228,577		Harold Sterling	34,037	
Richard Fulton	122,101				
• 1982 •					
Randy Tyree	318,205	500,937	Lamar Alexander	259,497	737,963
Anna B. O'Brien	254,500				

TABLE 5

Vote in Senatorial Elections since Implementation of Popular Election in 1916					
DEMOCRATIC PARTY			REPUBLICAN PARTY		
CANDIDATE	PRIMARY	GENERAL ELECTION	CANDIDATE	PRIMARY	GENERAL ELECTION
• 1916 •					
K. D. McKellar		143,719	Ben W. Hooper		118,174
• 1918 •					
John K. Shields	66,389	98,605	H. Clay Evans		59,989
Tom C. Rye	55,845				
• 1922 •					
K. D. McKellar	102,692	151,523	Newell Sanders	36,581	71,200
G. P. Fitzhugh	47,627		Harry Anderson	18,139	
• 1924 •					
L. D. Tyson	72,496	147,825	H. B. Lindsey		109,863
John K. Shields	54,990				
Nathan Bachman	44,946				
• 1928 •					
K. D. McKellar	120,298	175,431	James A. Fowler		120,289
Finis Garrett	64,470				
• 1930 • UNEXPIRED TERM					
William E. Brock	113,492	144,021	F. Todd Meacham		49,634
John R. Neal	47,110				
• 1930 • REGULAR TERM					
Cordell Hull	140,802	154,071	Paul E. Divine		58,550
Andrew L. Todd	79,549				
• 1934 • UNEXPIRED TERM					
Nathan Bachman	166,293		Dwayne Maddox	45,325	
Gordon Browning	121,169				
John R. Neal, Independent, polled 49,773 ballots in the general election. Maddox withdrew from the race.					
• 1934 • REGULAR TERM					
K. D. McKellar	unopposed	195,430	Ben W. Hooper	64,409	110,401
• 1936 •					
Nathan Bachman	217,531	273,298	Dwayne Maddox		69,753
John R. Neal	44,830				

continued

continued   **TABLE 5**

• 1938 •					
UNEXPIRED TERM					
Tom Stewart	174,940	194,028	Harley G. Fowler	11,760	72,098
George L. Berry	101,966				
J. Ridley Mitchell	70,393				
• 1940 •					
K. D. McKellar	230,033	295,440	Howard H. Baker		121,790
John R. Neal	14,630				
• 1942 •					
Tom Stewart	136,415	110,432	F. Todd Meacham		33,832
Edward W. Carmack	116,841				
• 1946 •					
K. D. McKellar	188,805	145,654	William Ladd	30,756	57,238
Edward W. Carmack	107,363				
• 1948 •					
Estes Kefauver	171,791	326,142	B. Carroll Reece	82,522	166,947
Tom Stewart	129,873				
John A. Mitchell	96,192				
• 1952 •					
Albert Gore	334,957	545,432	Hobert F. Atkins	25,061	153,479
K. D. McKellar	245,054				
• 1954 •					
Estes Kefauver	440,497	249,121	Ray II. Jenkins	45,015	
Pat Sutton	186,363		Tom Wall		106,971
Jenkins withdrew.					
• 1958 •					
Albert Gore	375,439	317,324	Hobert F. Atkins	23,714	76,371
Prentice Cooper	253,191				
• 1960 •					
Estes Kefauver	463,848	594,053	A. Bradley Frazier	16,633	234,053
Andrew T. Taylor	249,336		Hansel Profitt	11,667	
• 1964 •					
UNEXPIRED TERM					
Ross Bass	330,213	568,905	Howard Baker, Jr.	93,301	517,330
Frank G. Clement	233,245				
M. M. Bullard	86,718				
• 1964 •					
REGULAR TERM					
Albert Gore	401,163	570,542	Dan Kuykendall	72,376	493,475
Sam Galloway	37,974				
• 1966 •					
Frank G. Clement	384,322	383,843	Howard Baker, Jr.	112,617	483,063
Ross Bass	366,079				

continued

continued   **TABLE 5**

• 1970 •					
Albert Gore	269,770	519,858	William E. Brock	176,703	562,465
Hudley Crockett	238,767		Tex Ritter	54,401	

• 1972 •					
Ray Blanton	290,717	440,599	Howard Baker, Jr.	242,373	716,539
Don Palmer	40,600		Hubert D. Patty	7,581	

• 1976 •					
James Sasser	244,930	751,180	William E. Brock	173,743	673,231
John J. Hooker	171,716				
Harry Sadler	54,125				
David Bolin	44.056				

• 1978 •					
Jane Eskind	196,156	466,228	Howard Baker, Jr.	205,680	642,644
Bill Bruce	170,795		Harvey Howard	21,154	
J. D. Lee	89,939				

• 1982 •					
James Sasser	511,059	780,113	Robin Beard	205,271	479,642
Charles V. Vick	63,488		W. B. Thompson, Jr.	19,277	

• 1984 •					
Albert Gore, Jr.	345,527	991,312	Victor Ashe	145,744	553,331
			Jack McNeil	17,970	

Ed McAteer, Independent, polled 85,745 ballots in the general election.

Bibliographical Essay

This bibliographical essay is by no means complete or all-inclusive. A complete listing of all of the journal articles and monographs on the history of Tennessee and the South would consume an excessive amount of space. This essay does, however, contain most of those works from which fact has been obtained and basic interpretations drawn. It also contains all studies identified in the text.

Tennessee's past cannot be fully understood out of context of its regional identification. Those who wish to pursue in greater depth the history of Tennessee since the Civil War should begin by examining the history of the South. Three classic studies provide a valuable introduction to Southern history since the Civil War: C. Vann Woodward, *Origins of the New South, 1877-1913*, vol. 9 of *A History of the South* (Baton Rouge: Louisiana State University Press, 1951); George Brown Tindall, *The Emergence of the New South, 1913-1945*, vol. 10 of *A History of the South* (Baton Rouge: Louisiana State University Press, 1967); and Charles P. Roland, *The Improbable Era: The South Since World War II*, revised edition (Lexington: The University Press of Kentucky, 1976).

There is no end to the number of interpretative studies of the South but the following are especially valuable: Dewey W. Grantham, *The Democratic South* (Athens: University of Georgia Press, 1963); Dewey W. Grantham, *The Regional Imagination: The South and Recent American History* (Nashville: Vanderbilt University Press, 1979); Dewey W. Grantham, *Southern Progressivism: The Reconciliation of Progress and Tradition* (Knoxville: The University of Tennessee Press, 1983); George Brown Tindall, *The Ethnic Southerners*

(Baton Rouge: Louisiana State University Press, 1976); and George Brown Tindall, *The Persistent Tradition of Community in New South Politics* (Baton Rouge: Louisiana State University Press, 1975). Two valuable works providing insights into the modern South are Numan V. Bartley, *The Rise of Massive Resistance: Race and Politics in the South During the 1950s* (Baton Rouge: Louisiana State University Press, 1969) and Numan V. Bartley and Hugh Davis Graham, *Southern Politics and the Second Reconstruction* (Baltimore and London: The Johns Hopkins University Press, 1975). Useful are Jack Bass and Walter DeVries, *The Transformation of Southern Politics: Social Change and Political Consequence Since 1945* (New York: Basic Books, Incorporated, Publishers, 1976) and Neal R. Pierce, *The Border States South: People, Politics, and Power in the Five Border South States* (New York: W. W. Norton and Company, Incorporated, 1975). Although brief and perhaps superficial, James C. Cobb, *Industrialization and Southern Society, 1877-1984* (Lexington: The University Press of Kentucky, 1984) provides a valuable summary of Southern economic development since the Civil War.

The only up-to-date survey of Tennessee history is Robert E. Corlew, *Tennessee: A Short History*, second edition (Knoxville: The University of Tennessee Press, 1981). Lee Seifert Greene, David H. Grubbs, and Victor C. Hobday, *Government in Tennessee*, third edition (Knoxville: The University of Tennessee Press, 1975) is an excellent study of government and politics in the Volunteer State.

There are a number of volumes covering the military phase of the Civil War in Tennessee but a dearth on the occupation and governance. Peter Maslowski, *Treason Must Be Made Odious: Military Occupation and Wartime Reconstruction in Nashville, Tennessee, 1862-1886* (Millwood NY: KTO Press, 1978) partially fills the void. The era of Reconstruction is more than adequately covered in Thomas B. Alexander, *Political Reconstruction in Tennessee* (New York: Russell and Russell, 1968).

There is not an abundance of works on the Volunteer State since the Civil War. Those available, however, are well done. The state debt issue is ably chronicled by Robert B. Jones, *Tennessee at the Crossroads: The State Debt Controversy, 1870-1883* (Knoxville: The University of Tennessee Press, 1977). Joseph H. Cartwright, *The Triumph of Jim Crow: Tennessee Race Relations in the 1880s* (Knoxville:

The University of Tennessee Press, 1976) traces the difficulties of blacks in post-Reconstruction Tennessee. The political history of the state is the subject of Dan Robison, *Bob Taylor and the Agrarian Revolt in Tennessee* (Chapel Hill: University of North Carolina Press, 1935). The more recent Roger L. Hart, *Redeemers, Bourbons, and Populists: Tennessee, 1870-1896* (Baton Rouge: Louisiana State University Press, 1978) is more thoroughly researched. The chapters on Tennessee in Gordon McKinney, *Southern Mountain Republicans, 1865-1900: Politics and the Appalachian Community* (Chapel Hill: University of North Carolina Press, 1978) provides a brief history of the Republican party in East Tennessee.

Limited insights into the agrarian revolt, progressivism, and prohibition may be found in William R. Majors, *Editorial Wild Oats: Edward Ward Carmack and Tennessee Politics* (Macon: Mercer University Press, 1984). Paul E. Isaac, *Prohibition and Politics: Turbulent Decades in Tennessee, 1885-1920* (Knoxville: The University of Tennessee Press, 1965) is a well-done treatment of the prohibition movement in the state. The only authoritative study of progressivism in Tennessee is a dissertation, Joe Michael Shahan, "Reform and Politics in Tennessee: 1906-1914" (Ph.D. dissertation, Vanderbilt University). Progressivism in Memphis is described in William D. Miller's well-written *Memphis During the Progressive Era, 1900-1917* (Memphis: Memphis State University Press, 1957). Black history through the progressive era and beyond is traced in Lester C. Lamon, *Black Tennesseans, 1900-1930* (Knoxville: The University of Tennessee Press, 1977).

A study of the post-progressive era in Tennessee should include V. O. Key, Jr., "Tennessee: The Civil War and Mr. Crump," *Southern Politics in State and Nation* (New York: Alfred A. Knopf, 1949); David D. Lee, *Tennessee in Turmoil: Politics in the Volunteer State, 1920-1932* (Memphis: Memphis State University Press, 1979); John Berry McFerrin, *Caldwell and Company: A Southern Financial Empire* (Nashville: Vanderbilt University Press, 1969); William R. Majors, *The End of Arcadia: Gordon Browning and Tennessee Politics* (Memphis: Memphis State University Press, 1982); and William D. Miller, *Mr. Crump of Memphis* (Baton Rouge: Louisiana State University Press, 1964).

There is truly a dearth of monographic literature on Tennessee since World War II. Desegregation is traced in Hugh Davis Graham, *Crisis in Print: Desegregation in the Press in Tennessee* (Nashville: Vanderbilt University Press, 1967). Lee Seifert Greene, *Lead Me On: Frank Goad Clement and Tennessee Politics* (Knoxville: The University of Tennessee Press, 1982) tells the story of Governor Clement. Finally, Lee Seifert Green and Jack E. Holmes, "Tennessee: A Politics of Peaceful Change," *The Changing Politics of the South,* ed. William C. Havard (Baton Rouge: Louisiana State University Press, 1972) provides an interpretive view of Tennessee since World War II.

Index